Critical Issues in Education

MW00526251

Joseph Murphy, Series Editor

Developing Effective Principals Through Collaborative Inquiry
MÓNICA BYRNE-JIMÉNEZ AND MARGARET TERRY ORR

Distributed Leadership in Practice
JAMES P. SPILLANE AND JOHN B. DIAMOND, EDS.

Principal Accomplishments: How School Leaders Succeed
G. THOMAS BELLAMY, CONNIE L. FULMER, MICHAEL J. MURPHY, AND RODNEY MUTH

Balanced Leadership: How Effective Principals Manage Their Work
SHERYL BORIS-SCHACTER AND SONDRA LANGER

A New Agenda for Research in Educational Leadership
WILLIAM A. FIRESTONE AND CAROLYN RIEHL, EDS.

The Effective Principal: Instructional Leadership for High-Quality Learning
BARBARA SCOTT NELSON AND ANNETTE SASSI

Redesigning Accountability Systems for Education
SUSAN H. FUHRMAN AND RICHARD F. ELMORE, EDS.

Taking Account of Charter Schools: What's Happened and What's Next?
KATRINA E. BULKLEY AND PRISCILLA WOHLSTETTER, EDS.

Learning Together, Leading Together:
Changing Schools through Professional Learning Communities
SHIRLEY M. HORD, ED.

Who Governs Our Schools? Changing Roles and Responsibilities
DAVID T. CONLEY

School Districts and Instructional Renewal
AMY M. HIGHTOWER, MICHAEL S. KNAPP,
JULIE A. MARSH, AND MILBREY W. MCLAUGHLIN, EDS.

Effort and Excellence in Urban Classrooms:
Expecting—and Getting—Success with All Students
DICK CORBETT, BRUCE WILSON, AND BELINDA WILLIAMS

Developing Educational Leaders: A Working Model:
The Learning Community in Action
CYNTHIA J. NORRIS, BRUCE G. BARNETT, MARGARET R. BASOM, AND DIANE M. YERKES

Understanding and Assessing the Charter School Movement
JOSEPH MURPHY AND CATHERINE DUNN SHIFFMAN

School Choice in Urban America: Magnet Schools and the Pursuit of Equity
CLAIRE SMREKAR AND ELLEN GOLDRING

Lessons from High-Performing Hispanic Schools: Creating Learning Communities
PEDRO REYES, JAY D. SCRIBNER, AND ALICIA PAREDES SCRIBNER, EDS.

Schools for Sale: Why Free Market Policies
Won't Improve America's Schools, and What Will
ERNEST R. HOUSE

Reclaiming Educational Administration as a Caring Profession
LYNN G. BECK

DEVELOPING EFFECTIVE PRINCIPALS THROUGH COLLABORATIVE INQUIRY

Mónica Byrne-Jiménez
Margaret Terry Orr

Foreword by Tom Sobol

TEACHERS
COLLEGE
PRESS

Teachers College, Columbia University
New York and London

Published by Teachers College Press, 1234 Amsterdam Avenue, New York, NY 10027

Library of Congress Cataloging-in-Publication Data

Byrne-Jiménez, Mónica.
   Developing effective principals through collaborative inquiry / Mónica Byrne-Jiménez and Margaret Terry Orr ; foreword by Tom Sobol.
      p.   cm. — (Critical issues in educational leadership series)
   Includes bibliographical references and index.
   ISBN 978-0-8077-4816-9 (pbk : alk. paper) — ISBN 978-0-8077-4817-6 (cloth : alk. paper)
   1. School principals—United States.   2. Educational leadership—United States.   3. Group work in education—United States.   4. School management and organization—United States.   I. Orr, Margaret Terry, 1953–   II. Title.

   LB2831.93.B97 2007
   371.2'012—dc22

                                                                                        2007017637

ISBN: 978-0-8077-4816-9 (paper)
ISBN: 978-0-8077-4817-6 (cloth)

Printed on acid-free paper
Manufactured in the United States of America

14   13   12   11   10   09   08   07   8   7   6   5   4   3   2   1

Contents

Contents

Foreword

There are good schools with good principals, and there are bad schools with bad principals. In some places there may be bad schools with good principals. But nowhere are there good schools with bad principals. It is a settled matter that the leadership provided by principals is absolutely essential for schools of high quality.

There is such consensus on the point that one would expect corresponding agreement on how principals should be prepared for their jobs and nurtured while in them. But such is not the case. In many places professional development consists of top-down demands for better test scores, as if the shame and fear of low scores will bring about the leadership that is needed. Elsewhere, higher education institutions teach their academic courses, secure in the dubious assumption that what the faculty wants to teach is what the principals need to know. Only rarely do we find programs that integrate theory and practice, and design them to promote both individual growth and collective endeavor. As a rule, we do not apply to principals the principles of teaching and learning we hope to see in our teaching faculty and administrative staffs.

Into this morass stride Professors Byrne-Jiménez and Orr, doing everything right. Their program of Collaborative Inquiry is based on established principles of adult learning. It takes as its subject problems of practice in the learners' real work. Absent are the conventional a priori "solutions" to these problems—the solutions are the products of participants' knowledge and experience. (Think of

Donald Schön's "reflective practitioner" in a group setting.) The program fosters both individual learning and the learners' relationship to the group. It models in form what it wants in the schools. "How one learns," write the authors, "is closely related to how one leads."

The authors present their work with useful illustrations and straight talk. In the style of their CI program, they raise as many questions as they assert opinions. But the guidance they provide is lucid and straightforward. Here is a text that makes itself plain.

As most of us have learned, there is no one way to achieve our goals for education. But I have no doubt that future CI participants will agree that this is one way that works.

Tom Sobol
Teachers College, Columbia University

Acknowledgments

This book grew out of conversations and colleagueship among us and a New York City public school principal, Peter McFarlane, when we were all at Teachers College, Columbia University, as a faculty member, student, and graduate. We agreed then that higher education leadership preparation programs and even urban district leadership understood too little about the challenges and best strategies to effectively turn around low-performing schools. We were frustrated by the narrowness of school reform that reduces effective leadership and school improvement to a handful of strategies. We realized that rapid turnaround of low-performing schools was rare; yet it was the unquestioned demand of urban district leaders and state and federal accountability systems.

We decided to try out a new, untried approach to school improvement through leadership development, drawing upon the lived experiences of new principals charged with dramatically improving recently labeled "failed" schools. We had learned about collaborative inquiry through our faculty colleagues at Teachers College—Victoria Marsick and Lyle Yorks—who provided strong encouragement and were significant sounding boards as we developed our collaborative inquiry process. We were convinced that insights into and conclusions about effective school improvement would surface through this process. We were not wrong, and were rewarded with one of the richest professional learning experiences of our careers.

We are deeply indebted to the six principals who took a chance with us and with an untried professional learning opportunity. Their commitment and uncompensated participation over 18 months reaped significant rewards for them and us through the rich and dynamic conversations we held, the learning we all gained about effective school improvement, and the support we provided one another as we navigated hugely challenging problems and opportunities. Their thoughtfulness and reflection on both their journey and ours (as academics learning about their work and their leadership development) were invaluable.

This book would not have been possible without their time, commitment and thoughtfulness. We are particularly indebted to Peter McFarlane (Dr. Mac to his faculty and friends), who was the link that brought us all together, provided the space (and often food) for our meetings, and strongly encouraged us through the early sessions as we found our footing and developed the routines that became formalized as our collaborative inquiry process for leadership development.

We have since applied this model in other settings, with both principals and superintendents, reaffirming the dynamic learning that this process fosters. Through that work, we learned how applicable this model is for leadership development generally through both individual and collective problem solving. We have shared our work at several professional research forums, particularly the American Educational Research Association annual conferences, and thank our peers for their critical feedback on what we learned. Their insights and questions helped us think more deeply about how to explain this process for others to use.

As academic colleagues, the two of us were greatly enriched through this process, both professionally and personally. We share fond memories of our long walks to and from Peter's school, during which we tried to make sense of what we were learning, both about school leadership and about principal professional development. We honed the art of collaborative work—and friendship—for ourselves, making this book, and other shared professional writing possible.

Finally, this book would not have been possible without the encouragement, support, and counterbalances in our lives. For Monica, it has been her colleagues at UMass Boston and Hofstra University, who have been unwavering in their support, and her family, who listened patiently as she thought out loud. For Terry, it has been her colleagues at Bank Street College, where collaborative inquiry has become more central to her leadership preparation work, and her four sons, who constantly challenge her on the art of collaborative conversations.

CHAPTER 1

Overview

ONE PRINCIPAL'S BEGINNING

Matt pulled up to the curb in front of his new school, the Franklin Learning Academy. A quick perusal of the exterior gave him his first clue of the work that lay ahead. Used paper cups and sandwich wrappers littered the school grounds, while other windblown debris lined the school walls and corners. Blue graffiti was scrawled on the entrance walls, not incongruent with the barred windows and heavy steel doors. It looked more like a neglected prison than an inviting elementary school. While this was Matt's second school, it was to become a career-defining challenge. The school had achieved the distinction of being the worst-performing school in the district. Given what he could see and what he had experienced in improving schools, he knew he had his work cut out for him.

In his briefcase was the district's new plan for improving its lowest-performing schools through curriculum, instruction, and school governance. The plan mandated the adoption of a whole-school reform model, with staff training to be provided the day before school was to begin. The model had a tightly prescribed curriculum and instructional process for literacy and math education. The school was also to form a site-based management team for decision making and leadership advisement. Matt did not know what the school had been doing up until now. He anticipated, however, staff resistance to another new curriculum and instructional approach and the added time for team meetings and problem solving.

In his new office, a barren narrow space with a stainless-steel desk and file cabinets, he found a brand-new fax machine and computer. As he unpacked them, he mentally ran through his schedule for the week. First thing in the morning, he had to attend a 3-hour administrators meeting at the district office, across the county from his school. The technical-assistance representative for the whole-school reform model was coming in the afternoon to deliver the first batch of new instructional materials and talk through the upcoming schedule of training and meetings.

After setting up the fax machine, he put aside the boxes to walk through the building. The classrooms still needed their summer cleaning, and many bulletin boards still wore winter decorations, many teacher-made or purchased, rather than examples of student work. He could find few reading books for students in the classrooms aside from workbooks, and the library was a bleak hodgepodge of books and magazines.

Where to begin, whom to start with, and who would back him up, he wondered? At an earlier district administrative meeting, he had felt like an outsider. Other, older principals had sat bragging to one another about the new educational equipment they had purchased with their PTA-raised funds, a resource he did not anticipate having. While their schools were only a few blocks away, he did not think their schools were as large or their students as poor and mobile, and the achievement performances as low. His new superintendent had admitted that her experiences were primarily with more-middle-class schools and communities. Who would support him on issues of building maintenance, staff hiring and discipline, and garnering much needed resources and programs to get his school ready for the new reforms?

Returning to his office, he heard the click of the fax machine. Already there were four directives in the out tray, reminding him to file his building safety plan, to submit a list of teachers coming to the all-day whole-school reform model training, and (twice) to confirm his attendance at tomorrow's administrative meeting. He could not imagine, given the context, how there would be much discussion about leadership and school improvement at this meeting, only directions on what was to be done next.

Matt's scenario provides a snapshot of the complexity of principal leadership, particularly to improve low-performing schools and the kinds of leadership support and development needed, but often absent in schools and districts.

This chapter provides an overview on the need for principal leadership development by exploring in greater depth the current nature of the principalship, particularly for but not limited to urban principals, and current approaches and opportunities for principal leadership development. The need for alternative ways to support novice and experienced principals, particularly within urban contexts and accountability climates, points to the importance of an ongoing collaborative learning community of practice for continuous learning and reflection. It follows with an overview of collaborative inquiry and its use in a leadership seminar model as a powerful leadership development approach, as our research on this model shows.

This book is for people who work with principals and other school leaders. The book is designed to help them in adopting a more effective approach to professional development and use of administrative meeting time for principals' professional learning, by developing their capacity to learn and improve their practice together. This book is drawn from a research endeavor on how to foster principals' professional learning through collaboration and inquiry. While this leadership development model was designed with urban principals, it can be applicable to all principals and other educational leaders. It is most useful for districts with a critical number of school leaders, particularly new ones, who face challenges in improving their schools.

CHANGING EDUCATION, CHANGING LEADERSHIP

The nature of public education has seen dramatic change in recent years with corresponding shifts in the principalship and the work of school leaders. Accountability and testing in all areas and levels of public education put pressure on schools to improve student performance, leading to reform work in curriculum, instruction, and organization. It is now commonly accepted that the principalship is a complex and demanding job encompassing instructional, community, and visionary forms of leadership "in an atmosphere of constant, volatile change" (Institute for Educational Leadership [IEL], 2000, p. 4). Principals' work spans outside the school as well as in, with parents, community groups, and other government agencies. Such work must engage and focus combined efforts to help students improve their learning.

Several recent syntheses of research on educational leadership underscore the importance of school leadership on student achievement and the leadership qualities and practices that are most influential. Waters, Marzano, and McNulty (2003) identified 21 qualities that were most highly correlated with positive leadership impacts. Most important among these are being aware of the details and undercurrents of the school and using this in problem solving, making use of the most current theories and practices in education in working with faculty, distributing leadership among teachers on important matters, and being willing to actively challenge the status quo. The authors stress, however, that there is no one best way to improve schools and that principals must focus most on the change strategies that have the greatest impact on student achievement. Finally, they explain that leadership effectiveness is somewhat situational, highly dependent upon the dispositions and capacity for change of their school staff and community.

Leithwood and Riehl (2003) concluded in their research synthesis that educational leaders work in complex and changing environments with increasing requirements from policy directives, curriculum and assessment standards, and programmatic expectations. They also must respond to diverse student characteristics related to culture, income, disabilities, and learning capacities. On the basis of their research review, the authors define leadership as having two core functions—providing direction and exercising influence. Leaders, they explain, primarily work through and with others and create the conditions that enable others to be effective in their work. Thus, the basics of school leaders are in three broad categories— setting direction (through high expectations, developing shared goals, monitoring performance, and communication), developing people (through stimulation, support, and modeling) and developing the organization (by strengthening the school culture, organizational structuring, and collaborative processes and by managing the environmental pressures and opportunities).

Now more than ever, much of principals' job success depends upon the speed with which they can foster school improvement and accomplish student performance gains. Principals find themselves caught in the intersection of the pace and developmental nature of change (which requires 3–5 years at minimum, according to Fullan, 1991), and external policy expectations of more rapid progress. In addition, navigating among often competing perspectives about the form and approach to school improvement can be treacherous even for the most experienced leaders.

Hall and Hord (2001), in their research on educational change, showed that different leadership approaches influence the quality and effectiveness of implementation progress. Those leaders who most effectively implemented change had strongly held visions; in addition, they were motivators and fair-and-balanced problem solvers and were focused on student work as well as guided by their strong beliefs in good schools and teaching. In contrast, principals who were simply managers or responders to change might help implement what was directed but did not do more and, consequently, accomplished much less. Thus, possessing and using vision, passion, energy, and consistency make a difference in the quality of school improvement.

Given these findings, how can principals, particularly new ones, develop and sustain these qualities and enact them effectively to facilitate school improvement and improved student achievement?

THE CHALLENGES OF THE URBAN SCHOOL PRINCIPALSHIP

For urban school principals, there are additional leadership challenges. Urban districts are more often rated as challenging environments, with larger bureaucratic systems, less local revenue, and higher percentages of students living in poverty and having English as their second language (Crosby, 1999; NCES, 2001). Consequently, principals of urban schools reported greater job pressures, were more engaged in coordination of noninstructional supports, and played a greater role in mediating hopelessness and frustrations in comparison with their colleagues in nonurban schools (Portin, 2000).

It is not surprising, then, that urban schools are often plagued by principal shortages, particularly the poorest-performing ones, as the result of high rates of retirement and attrition and a reluctance of new candidates to fill available positions (IEL, 2000; Price, 1999). Consequently, many urban schools are led by principals who are new to both the role and the challenges of turning around low-performing schools. The federal No Child Left Behind Act and its pressure on all schools to demonstrate "annual yearly progress" in meeting high standards of student performance are pushing urban principals to accomplish what few have been able to do: dramatically improve student performance or face their own removal and their schools' reconstitution after 5 years (Craciun & Snow-Renner, 2002; Learning First Alliance, 2003).

In our collaborative inquiry on the urban principalship (Orr, Byrne-Jimenez, McFarlane, & Brown, 2005), the principals' descriptions of their schools reflected national characterizations of urban, low-performing schools as underresourced and challenged by years of staff and facility neglect, while facing high expectations for growth in student performance levels. The principals seemed to regard their schools contexts as givens, not challenges, and to some extent were familiar to them because of their prior work as teachers and subordinate school administrators. They were well aware of the role that the schools play in their communities and the importance of their work for them. They learned early in their principalships that their schools needed leadership to repair their facilities and problems, inspire a belief among the staff and school community in their capacity to improve, transform how they and their staff work on student learning, and protect their school from too many external demands and continuous change. They worked on many inter-related problems that complicated their school improvement efforts, such as safety, security, and facility improvement, while overcoming the demoralization of being labeled as a failed school. The complexity and relentlessness of these challenges made the principals hungry for opportunities to share their experiences and garner new ideas and strategies, while they were also wary of simple solutions or single-model reforms that left them with little latitude to adapt them to their schools.

Learning change-initiating leadership specifically does not come easily, particularly for those in urban areas, and often this is gained through trial and error on-the-job experience. Neufeld (1997), in interviews of 23 urban middle school principals about their training and support needs for school reform, concluded that the principals had to do significant work to transform themselves into leaders. This entailed reconstructing core ideas about their role and "how they should spend their time, set their priorities, seek new knowledge and skills, and situate themselves with respect to teachers and others in the educational community" (p. 507).

PRINCIPAL AND DISTRICT RELATIONSHIPS

Much of principals' professional learning, beyond graduate preparation, comes from how they are socialized by their districts for their roles and from district-prescribed professional learning and administrative meetings. For new principals, these learning opportunities are critical to their development as they progress from "survival" to educational leadership and professional actualization (Parkay, Currie, & Rhodes, 1992).

Districts vary in their capacity to support their principals' ongoing leadership development, particularly when new. In an in-depth study of 12 new urban principals, Osterman and Sullivan (1996) found that principals' sense of efficacy—the internal capacity to be leaders through flexibility, collaboration, and persistence—was greatly influenced by their superiors as well as their subordinates. The more reasonable and clear the district's expectations, the convergence of goals and commitment, the organizational support and performance feedback, and the opportunities for communication and collaboration, the greater the principals' sense of efficacy.

Typically, districts provide support by prescribing strategies and accountability expectations. Among the principals in our collaborative inquiry on urban school leadership (Orr et al., 2005), the central district prescribed the school reform model: implementing new instructional programs, curriculum, and related professional development; reorganizing the school and its governance structure; and adding new staff and functions. District officials relied on tight organizational controls—through narrowly prescribed school improvement strategies, performance measures, and close administrative monitoring—to promote organizational improvement. Yet mandates and controls were woefully insufficient. The principals voiced a strong need for support in interpreting the district's reform model to fit their school's history and experiences and to shift from principal-directed to more collaborative leadership, to support the reforms. Moreover, the principals were most challenged by their lack of support—and were even restricted—to facilitate change in a manner that would engage and enhance staff and school capacity.

PRINCIPAL DEVELOPMENT: LEARNING THE PRINCIPALSHIP

New strategies and approaches may be necessary to enable principals to become more effective as school leaders and as part of larger districts to achieve academic improvement in resource-challenged environments. Such strategies require new, more effective forms of leadership development, many of which can be drawn from research in leadership development in education and elsewhere and adult learning theory generally. Such research stresses the importance of collaborative and supportive processes to foster personal growth, leadership efficacy, and organizational capacity generally.

In recent years the emphasis on, and need for, different ways of approaching principal learning and professional development has grown as efforts to improving student achievement have shifted to messier processes of school restructuring and related changes in educational leadership (Daresh & Playko, 1992). Various analyses of principal professional development are criticized for their lack of availability or inappropriate content and learning strategies (e.g., Hallinger & Wimpelberg, 1992; IEL, 2000; Walker, Mitchel, & Turner, 1999). For the urban principals in our inquiry (Orr et al., 2005), their professional development was primarily characterized as "fair warning" of what they would now be held accountable to, rather than as designed for capacity building or skill development.

Current recommendations and approaches for principal leadership development stress reflective, contextualized, collaborative ongoing learning (Bezzina, 1994; Hallinger & Wimpelberg, 1992). Portin (2000) recommends that content focus on issues specific to their context, such as "leveraging resources, communicating and understanding the needs of their community, and the ability to serve as a hub for multiple social services" (p. 504). Peterson (2001) advises that it be designed to "build skills and knowledge, enhance the flow of leaders to the principalship, develop a strong set of values and ethics, and enhance the ability to implement school improvement strategies" (p. 6).

More innovative principal development models are needed, models that embrace a more constructivist approach and build on, rather than underestimate, the skills and knowledge that principals already possess. Principal professional development should be about leadership—rather than introduce change solutions—and should include processes that enhance learning and capacity building, rather than simply transmission of knowledge. Moreover, such professional development should be woven into district socialization and supervision practices for principals, not stand apart, creating more coherence in leadership development for educational improvement (for principal socialization, see Hart, 1993).

Analyses of existing and exemplary principal professional development suggest critical attributes—that it be context based, incorporate reflection, and be undertaken collaboratively and over time. Three key approaches are reflective practice, structured conversations, and collaboration in learning.

Osterman and Kottkamp (2004) argue that reflective practice is an important professional development strategy, particularly in support of school reform. When combined with collaborative data-based inquiry and problem-solving conversations, it is both individually and organizationally meaningful. For individuals, it has the potential to renew one's sense of optimism, commitment, and efficacy, through support. Collectively, it has the potential to foster professional learning communities.

Structured professional conversations are often used in professional development to facilitate such deep, reflective learning. Reflective tools and discussion protocols can facilitate transformative learning for educators and educational leaders. McDonald, Mohr, Dichter, and McDonald (2003) showed how to use various protocols to structure discussion, problem solving, and learning about teaching and learning, based on the idea that knowledge is socially constructed—that "encounters with other people's understanding enable learners to gain and deepen their own understanding" (p. 7). Learning in this manner also teaches the value of diverse ideas and deliberative communities (McDonald et al., 2003).

Optimally, this learning is done in collaboration with others and incorporates facilitating learning structures and processes to create what Wenger (1998) calls a community of learners. Working through an intentional learning community can both foster and sustain reflective learning, especially in learning a new role (Lave & Wenger, 1991; Wenger, 1998). Situating learning in a community enables each learner to become acculturated in his or her knowledge community—learning both the formal expert knowledge and the expected norms and behaviors.

DEVELOPING COLLABORATIVE INQUIRY AS LEADERSHIP DEVELOPMENT

We combined these approaches in creating the Collaborative Inquiry Leadership Seminar as a dual learning strategy—to learn about the urban principalship and to foster leadership development. We were familiar with Reason's (1988) cooperative inquiry and the co-research dynamic of collaborative-action research (Greenwood & Levin, 1998; Sagor, 1992). We believed that this inquiry process would be useful as professional development, enabling principals to learn about and through one another, as we were, about the urban principalship and effective strategies for improving schools.

Our strategy took form when we begin the seminar as a pilot program with six principals who dedicated their after-work time and building space for meetings. We sometimes brought food and drinks, and occasionally dinner, while talking for 2–3 hours in the late afternoon and early evenings, meeting every 2–3 weeks over 18 months. We were explicit with the principals about the newness of our approach, our hope for learning, and our anticipation of the process as professional development. While initially wary of what would occur, the principals quickly grew to look forward to the sessions to update one another on their experiences and to reflect on their work. Through our facilitation and discussion with the principals, we gradually developed a structure for our discussions as inquiry into practice and reflection on their meaning. We judiciously drew in relevant research and theoretical literature, learning to apply and criticize as warranted. Over time, we shared what we had learned about how we were learning, gaining feedback and furthering our reflection.

THE COLLABORATIVE INQUIRY LEADERSHIP SEMINAR

The Collaborative Inquiry Leadership Seminar, as we developed it, follows a fairly simple process. Over time, we incorporated features of Marsick's (2002) action-learning conversation protocol and the collaborative-inquiry-in-practice process used by Bray, Lee, Smith, and Yorks (2000) to further structure and enhance our inquiry process. Our inquiry began with an overarching question: How can principals effectively improve their schools and student achievement? In our seminar process, regular meetings are held among a common and sustained group of committed participants, using a structured protocol to facilitate participation, questions, and reflection about problems of practice that relate to the larger question. After a brief period in which participants update one another on events that had transpired since the previous meeting, the group selects a problem or situation for discussion—usually one that is urgent, complex, or common among the ones raised. The problem holder (the person who presented the problem) briefly elaborates on the problem or situation, providing details about the history, the persons involved, and related concerns. Next, while the problem holder remains quiet, each participant asks clarifying questions. After the problem holder addresses these questions, the participants take turns surfacing assumptions and reframing the problem or situation, often drawing on their own similar experiences. The problem holder then reframes the problem as well, using some of the new insights. After further discussion with the problem holder, participants recommend solutions that are framed by their perspective on the problem. The problem holder is given time to reflect upon the suggestions and propose his or her planned course of action. The facilitator asks guiding questions, monitors discussion and questioning time, and helps to summarize and give feedback to the group intermittently to stimulate further discussion.

The Collaborative Inquiry Leadership Seminar is so termed to reflect its four core elements: who is learning, what is learned, how learning occurs, and the conditions for learning. First, it is collaborative. Participating educational leaders and facilitators are co-learners, who create a trusting, confidential learning environment. Those who participate must be committed to their own learning and to supporting the learning of others. This means having an openness to question one's own assumptions and practices, an interest in learning from others' experiences, and a commitment to continuous learning for improvement. Consequently, it assumes that participants bring knowledge and experience that can enhance others' learning and problem solving, particularly when pooled in collaborative work.

Second, it is about leadership and its improvement. It assumes that leadership is itself an ongoing learning process, through learning by doing (as is stressed by the Center for Creative Leadership, as described by McCauley, Moxley, & Van Velsor, 1998). It also assumes that leadership can be developed and enhanced and that existing organizational practices can be improved through reflection, discussion, and problem solving. It acknowledges that leadership encompasses many challenges and novel dilemmas for which ready solutions or strategies are not apparent and for which new learning is appropriate. Thus, it is framed around a driving question about leadership effectiveness in the work of school improvement and student achievement.

Third, it uses inquiry to facilitate learning. Inquiry incorporates the processes of data gathering, hypothesis formulation, assumption questioning, and alternative generation in a cyclical learning process. Inquiry exists at two levels—into the problems each participant brings for discussion and into the larger question that frames the inquiry itself. Through the process of characterizing his or her own problems and challenges, an individual begins to unearth problem dimensions and assumptions. By listening to others as they reframe these same situations from their own perspectives, individuals learn to consider alternative hypotheses and assumptions and to generate alternative actions. With an ongoing seminar structure, all participants have opportunities to follow up on problems and scenarios as they unfold over time, to learn about the consequences of solutions tried, and to propose new alternatives or reframing. Further, the seminar process provides an opportunity to reflect upon the participants' collective learning over time, in answer to the overarching question.

Fourth, it is structured as a seminar to provide focus and support. The discussions are conducted in a democratic, seminar style, in which the participants actively talk, with modest facilitation. The seminar structure offers a means of exploring and learning constructively from challenging situations and dilemmas by turning these into learning opportunities and using agreed-upon protocols to structure questioning, discussing, and reflecting.

When the elements are used together, the Collaborative Inquiry Leadership Seminar creates a professional learning community among the participants that transcends the seminar itself, leading to formal and informal relationships beyond the seminar sessions. The participants gain confidential colleagues with whom they can consult and share experiences and with whom they have a common language.

For participating educational leaders, the Collaborative Inquiry Leadership Seminar can provide a variety of lessons. At the very least, sharing problems and challenges enables participants to pool their knowledge of schools and of district and community expectations for their leadership and school improvement work. Through one another, they gain access to new ideas, strategies, and practices—because of their individual exposure through other preparatory and professional experiences—to be incorporated into their own work. Participants also gain alternative ways of framing problems and situations. As Bolman and Deal (1997) articulate, leaders often approach problems from one or two common frames of reference, among these structural, human relations, political, and symbolic. Leaders who are effective problem solvers are able to adapt their frames of reference (Leithwood & Steinbach, 1995). Learning to use different frames as shared by peer principals enables leaders to construct a more comprehensive means of interpreting problems and generating solutions.

Much of the discussions in the Collaborative Inquiry Leadership Seminar center on the challenges within the participants' work—fostering school improvement and facilitating organizational change. Thus, participants gain new insight into what and how they can do to improve student learning through their school's organization, instructional practices, and the way in which school staff work together. Eventually, such discussions evolve into reflections on the nature of leadership, providing opportunities for comparing and contrasting participants' approaches and consequences and looking at ways of improving their leadership, often through development of more transformational leadership practices (Leithwood & Jantzi, 1999). These reflections evolve into appreciative inquiry, looking at success and understanding what works (see Cooperrider & Whitney, 2005). Finally, the collaborative inquiry process becomes a learning experience itself, as participating leaders begin using the process among their faculty to facilitate inquiry for individual and organizational learning.

OUR INQUIRY ABOUT THIS FORM
OF LEADERSHIP DEVELOPMENT

The collaborative inquiry leadership seminar approach described in this book is an outgrowth of this 18-month seminar experience, and our subsequent replication of the model in other settings and with other leadership audiences. In this initial seminar, the group grappled with one guiding question, How do I do my job better—to lead and improve a low performing school? and later added another question, How do I learn to lead better and how can I learn leadership with others?

Throughout the collaborative inquiry cycle, the discussions were taped and transcribed (with the group's permission) and the two researchers kept discussion notes. At the end of 18 months, the six principals were interviewed in depth about the discussions, their personal backgrounds, and how they learned about the principalship. The meeting notes, transcripts, and follow-up interviews were analyzed using qualitative content analysis techniques, particularly for grounded theory (Miles & Huberman, 1994; Strauss & Corbin, 1990) and focus group data analysis techniques (Krueger, 1994) to develop themes and relationships.

Our learning was complex and iterative (Byrne-Jiménez & Orr, 2004). The problems that participants presented, we learned, were actually vehicles for larger questions and learning about their roles and their leadership, in addition to the more concrete demands of the job. The kind of learning in the group progressed over the 18 months from concrete problem solving to the development of more abstract problem-solving frameworks, to forming leadership approaches. Over time, participants became more and more sophisticated in their inquiry and analysis of one another's problems and seeing implications for their own work.

We facilitators found—and the principals agreed—that the principals gained five types of learning through the collaborative inquiry: organizational knowledge about rules, regulations, their interpretation, and normative expectations; new professional practice ideas (such as new models of staff development); new perspectives for problem framing; educational improvement and change; and leadership. In addition, the collaborative inquiry process itself was a learning outcome—learning how to spend more time on problem exploration and investigation and helping others consider solutions rather than simply solving the problem for them.

The collaborative inquiry experience affected the participants in many ways, both direct and indirect. Directly, it improved their leadership practice. Indirectly, however, it changed them, their leadership, and how they worked with one another. Specifically, the participants came to value their collaborative inquiry experience in terms of their practice and socialization, personal development, and creation of a support system. Not everyone participated to the same extent or gained the same kinds of learning through the process. Nonetheless, all voiced a shared value of the opportunity to share challenges in their work in a safe and supportive environment, and all learned to anticipate how others would encourage them to frame their problems. Some began to use the collaborative inquiry model in their work with their school communities to engage others in problem framing and solving and to develop new leadership roles for teachers. Some also tried out new practice ideas (i.e., teacher professional development), which they had learned from the group, and could reflect on with the group at subsequent sessions.

The six principals were primarily from state-designated low-performing schools in one urban district and are somewhat demographically similar to urban principals nationwide.[1] One was from a semiurban school district. Most were in their early to midcareers as administrators and intended to advance further in educational leadership. Together, they have worked in several community districts and school settings in teaching and administrative capacities. During our time together, four schools made dramatic gains in reading performance between school years 2000 and 2002, and three made similar dramatic gains in math performance. One school covered grades PK–2 and had no standardized testing, and the other was slated to be closed and eventually was. By school year 2003, four schools were removed from state review, and three principals had been recognized as principals of the year for their dramatic school improvement work.

ORGANIZATION OF THE BOOK

The book is organized around the collaborative inquiry process and its impact on principals' learning and leadership. In Chapter 2, we explain the Collaborative Inquiry Leadership Seminar in terms of the process within and across seminars. Chapter 3 provides a theoretical background to the Collaborative Inquiry Leadership Seminar, in terms of the quality attributes of professional development, adult learning theory, socialization theory, and leadership development. In Chapter 4, we outline the process of forming a collaborative inquiry group from its inception, to its evolving questions, to its ultimate conclusion. In Chapter 5, we describe the role of the facilitator, both as co-inquirer and as structuring and supporting the inquiry. Chapter 6 provides a conclusion and reflection for the book.

The book also includes three appendixes: case vignettes of selected issues that were the basis for discussion among the group, as illustration of the complexity of the leadership challenges and the dynamics of the inquiry; process guidelines for conducting the collaborative inquiry as professional development; and process guidelines for conducting the collaborative inquiry as a research methodology.

AUDIENCE

This book is designed for leadership development academics and practitioners, school district officials who foster professional development, faculty of leadership preparation programs, collaborative inquiry experts, and adult educators generally. Districts, particularly urban ones with large numbers of schools and school principals, are using leadership development as a primary reform approach. This leadership development model, we believe, provides a powerful, but low-cost, form of ongoing professional learning that improves both individual and district capacity for learning leadership and reflecting on leadership practice.

FINAL THOUGHT

What our experiences have shown through the collaborative inquiry process is that it requires two levels of commitment to learning—the commitment of the participants as co-inquirers—and the commitment of a district to support the learning and its application as new or modified leadership and organizational practices. Those who actively participated throughout seemed to gain the most personally and organizationally. In the replication of this work and in observing similar forms of collaborative inquiry for leadership development, we have concluded that district support is essential. It facilitates both learning and application of solutions to the leaders' work and makes learning more central to how leaders work together.

The Collaborative Inquiry Leadership Seminar: Description and Examples

> We gather in the school library, rearranging the tables into a conference table big enough for all of us to sit around comfortably. Someone sets snacks and drinks in the center for all to share. The two facilitators sit among the principals, who chat amicably about a recent administrative meeting they had attended. When the last person arrives, the informal discussion winds down and the collaborative inquiry begins.

This chapter provides a succinct description of how to select a collaborative inquiry question, the components of the collaborative inquiry leadership seminar, and how it works within each session and over time as a series of integrated discussions. Each collaborative inquiry leadership seminar follows a similar process, although the seminars evolve in their focus over time. At its core, collaborative inquiry is a structured process for problem understanding and solution generation, with defined roles and pacing for questioning and solution suggestions. Its pacing enables participants to offer and gain new insights and direction. While facilitators and participants have positional roles in the process, they also have a shared role as inquirers and learners, creating a sense of trust and capacity building. We examine the following key ideas:

- Collaborative inquiry is framed by an overarching question, within which problems of practice are explored and problem-solving approaches identified.
- There are four aspects to problem solving: problem identification, problem exploration, solution generation, and solution development.
- Complex problems require multiple frames of reference that can unpack their elements and generate novel solutions.
- Educational leaders often rely on one or two frames of reference for problem solving and can benefit from others' frames to provide new insights and solutions.
- Structured reflection with colleagues can facilitate better problem understanding and solutions; it is a skill that can be developed through practice.

SELECTING A COLLABORATIVE INQUIRY FRAMING QUESTION

The collaborative inquiry begins and is framed by a shared question of interest. When used in principal professional development, the collaborative inquiry question is often framed around questions of leadership and organizational effectiveness—such as *How best to lead change?* or *What leadership practices best facilitate school performance and student achievement?*

It is important that participants understand that this form of professional development is founded on an inquiry question. This sets the tone for the overall process as one of joint learning—rather than the delivery of information or strategies, as is more typical of conventional professional development. As such, participants have a role in shaping and committing to the initial framing question. Over time, the question may shift or be redefined as the group learns to work together and surface shared issues of importance that sharpen the group's inquiry orientation.

Such a question establishes an overarching motivation for the group's engagement and a focal point for reflection and action. It also serves to shift the focus of professional development to one of continuous learning, meaning making, and application, rather than the transmission of information and directions for action.

SEMINAR COMPONENTS

Each collaborative inquiry seminar is unique, but all seminars consist of five primary components:

- *Problem sharing.* Sharing a problem of practice and selecting a problem for discussion
- *Problem exploration.* Discussing the problem, using a protocol-framed process
- *Problem reframing.* Proposing different ways of interpreting the problem by raising unexamined assumptions
- *Problem solving.* Proposing different types of solutions based on different frames.
- *Problem solving applications.* Integrating different solution ideas based on reframing and considering their implications as organizational change

Sharing and selecting a problem. The first part of the inquiry is sharing problems of practice and then selecting one problem for discussion. The focus of the inquiry is to explore and solve a complex issue or problem of leadership practice. Through the deep exploration and analysis of one problem, participants learn how to use multiple perspectives to understand a problem and generate several plausible solutions. All participants learn more about complex problem solving generally by working on multiple problems, both theirs and others. The learning begins, however, through an in-depth analysis of one problem.

Selecting a problem for focused discussion (outlined in Figure 2.1) is a shared responsibility among inquiry members. To start the process, each participating principal shares a current problem of practice in a round-robin fashion. Each participant provides a brief

Figure 2.1. How to select a good problem for discussion: Features of fruitful problems.

Urgency

Scope

Implications for others in the group

Complexity

Uniqueness (had not been discussed before)

---

description of a problem, in 2 to 3 minutes, without answering questions or elaborating. The purpose is to provide just enough detail for the group to understand the problem and decide whether to select it as the focus for follow up.

> The group members quickly go around the room, sharing what is on their mind, or their current problem. "I have a teacher who will only sit in the front of the classroom to teach, and she has a first-grade class!" one principal exclaims despairingly. Another principal shares his worry that the district office will take over vacant building space for another program, adversely affecting his school. A third principal explains that a teacher she had not recommended for tenure had been positively approved by the superintendent and will continue to teach in her school. The principal laments how demoralized she feels, but needs to keep up a strong front until she has her own tenure review later this year. A fourth principal gives the group an update on the upcoming school community vote about whether to convert the school into a privately managed school charter. The group decides quickly to focus on this issue, because of its time sensitivity and stress.

After each participant shares a problem or issue, the group decides which problem should be a priority for that seminar's discussion. Some examples are detailed in Figure 2.2. Typically, the group gravitates toward a problem that is urgent or time sensitive and has applicability to others' situations and concerns. Sometimes, the group

Figure 2.2. Typical topics for collaborative inquiry.

Motivating a resistant teacher while navigating
related union and contract constraints

Learning to use a leadership team and constructively delegating
responsibilities while coordinating the quality of work

Handling invasive reporters who want to capture a
current school dilemma (such as security breaches)

Maintaining a productive and supportive working relationship
with central office personnel

Negotiating district directives while pursuing your
school improvement strategy

Planning for career advancement

Working constructively with demanding parents

Learning to take constructive feedback from superiors and peers
particularly in navigating district relations

---

recommends following up on a problem brought up by a member who has not had a problem discussed yet.

Discussing the problem. After selecting one problem, the group uses a structured discussion format to dig in more deeply to the problem's complexity, its underlying elements, and its relationship to organizational conditions, problems and priorities. This is a four-step process (outlined in Figure 2.3) in which (1) the problem holder elaborates on the problem, giving more background details and concerns about options and implications; (2) the other group members take turns in a round-robin question process to discuss the problem among themselves without the problem holder's comments; (3) the problem holder discusses the collective questions and insights raised by the group members; and (4) the group members

Figure 2.3. Problem discussion format.

Problem identification (10-15 minutes)

Discussing the problem

    1. Problem elaboration (15 minutes)

    2. Problem exploration (15-20 minutes)

    3. Reframing the problem (10 minutes)

    4. Assumption generation (5 minutes)

Problem solving

    1. Solution exploration (15-20 minutes)

    2. Solution selection (10 minutes)

    3. Considering implications and actions (10 minutes)

---

raise assumptions that they might make (or think the problem holder is making) about the problem or situation or assumptions.

During problem elaboration, the problem holder elaborates further on his or her problem for about 15 minutes. The speaker then gives more details about the problem and its context and shares his or her concerns and options being considered, such as describing stakeholders, the chronology of events, defining moments, and unintended consequences.

Next, the other group members explore the problem among themselves, offering their own insight into and wonderings about the problem itself. Through a round-robin series of questions and comments, the other participants each take a turn to explore the problem from their perspective. During this comment period, the problem holder does not engage in a back-and-forth response with each participant but remains silent. To share the discussion time, the participants take turns raising one or two points each initially, before passing on the discussion to the next person. The facilitators invite the participants to go around again until all questions and observations are made.

The problem holder takes a few minutes to give the group an update on the current situation. The press coverage has heightened
the tensions in the school and community over the possible charter
school takeover, as the mayor and superintendent lobby for it and
the private company pressures the community with promises of new
instructional resources. The group raises several questions from several vantage points: Has the staff discussed what is going on? What
does the staff think they will need to do differently if the community
votes down the charter school plan? How has this situation affected
instruction? The problem holder responds by saying that the staff is
unified and that they can improve the school, but have not demon-
strated any action. She is particularly concerned about the inac-
tion of "slackers" who are not tightening up their performance now
when they need to do it the most. She also feels unprepared to
navigate the many layers of politics and worries about the impact
of how students do on the upcoming standardized tests given all
the distractions.

During this problem exploration, participants may offer insights
or raise questions about the problem that shift the focus from details about the problem as initially posed to the broader organizational and policy context of the problem. In addition, the questioning
will help to surface underlying concerns and fears of the problem
holder that are based on broader organizational circumstances. Such
questions can probe elements such as

- *Temporal.* What is important about the timing of this problem?
- *History.* Has this problem or a similar problem occurred before? What solutions were tried before and what were the
  consequences?
- *Structure.* What organizational structures contribute to this
  problem or are affected by this problem?
- *Policy.* What organizational policies constrain your options?
  Contributed to causing this problem? Offer guidance on
  solutions?
- *Roles.* Who else is responsible for this problem and how? Who
  else could be involved in solving the problem? What would
  be the consequence of involving others?

- *Impact*. What does this problem affect? What are the ramifications of this problem? What impact is the problem holder anticipating for the solutions being considered?
- *Feelings*. How does this problem make the problem holder feel? What consequences does the problem holder fear?

The problem holder then takes a few minutes to respond to some of the questions and observations raised by the group members. During this time, this problem holder will provide new information and insight and offer more on his or her perspective on the problem under discussion.

In the last round of questioning, the group members take turns describing the assumptions that they might make ("If I were in your position, I might assume . . .") or assumptions that they think the problem holder is making ("When I hear you say . . . it sounds like you are assuming . . .").[1] Each person has a set of assumptions, beliefs, or theories-in-use that directly influence their actions. According to Osterman and Kottkamp (2004), the use of reflective practice to surface these assumptions is critical to changing how one addresses problems or sets new directions for action.

Such assumption questioning helps to move the discussion from its elements to the frameworks with which the problem holder (and each group member) is using to interpret the problem. By focusing on the assumptions, the problem holder and other group members can begin create different windows on the problem and how some assumptions may be contributing to the problem or limiting solution ideas. By surfacing some assumptions, the problem holder and group members may begin to see new opportunities for how to focus on the problem and its solution.

> Group members surface several assumptions: It sounds like you are assuming you have to solve this problem by yourself . . . It sounds like you are assuming that there are only negative consequences to this problem, when it may represent opportunities to leverage resources . . .

Reframing the problem. This is an important turning point in the collaborative discussion. It reflects how and in what ways the problem holder gains insight from the problem exploration discussion and the assumptions raised. The problem holder, after reflecting for a few moments on the questions, insights, and assumptions raised, restates the problem. A more informal discussion might ensue among the group members as they and the problem holder reach problem clarification at this juncture.

Again, each group member will take turns, in a round-robin, to reframe the problem. Often, group members will reframe the problem from their own preferred vantage point. Bolman and Deal's (1997) four-frame perspective on organizational behavior is a useful typology of commonly raised perspectives—politics and power; interpersonal relationships and human resource considerations; roles, structures, and systems; and organizational culture and symbolic meanings.

The problem discussion phase of the collaborative inquiry ends as the problem holder generates his or her own problem reframing, drawing, perhaps, on how the group members reframed the problem.

> The group members suggest several ways in which to reframe the problem: First, you are not in this alone; consider who is with you and create a sense of "we" within the school and within the broader professional community. Second, this is an organizational-change opportunity; use it as an opportunity to strengthen and focus on instructional change and improvement, through team building. Third, this is symbolically critical; consider the symbolic importance of this event as indication of community support and the school's promise to the community that can be harnessed. Fourth, this is a political opportunity; think about how to use the new political and district attention to garner new resources for the school.

Solving the problem. A similar discussion cycle is used for solving the problem, focusing now on the reframed problem. Understanding a problem better is only part of solving it effectively. Typically, collaborative inquiry participants have considerable practical experience and knowledge to inform problem solving. Through a collaborative process of exploring possible solutions, the problem holder can be guided to identify multiple solutions to the presenting problem and its underlying dimensions, to consider the opportunity to simultaneously address other related problems, and to identify policy and structural issues to be considered. Problem solving, like problem identification, is usually framed by one's preferred way of viewing organizational problems and assumptions about leadership practice. By learning multiple approaches to problem solving, the problem holder (and the other group members as well) gains other perspectives and orientations, thereby broadening his or her leadership repertoire. This is a two-step process of exploring possible solutions and developing a solution and action steps for the problem posed by the problem holder:

> *Solution exploration.* Through a second round-robin series of comments and observations, the participants provide suggestions to the problem holder on how to solve the problem as clarified. In this cycle, the participants share what has worked for them, what they have observed working or not working in similar situations, and what policy and structures might shape their suggestions. Again, each participant speaks for only a few minutes before passing the discussion on to the following person. Often, each participant builds on the suggestions of the prior speaker, shaping and extending a solution or set of solution strategies. Or conversely, a participant may present a distinctly different approach, in juxtaposition to the suggestions raised by other group members.
>
> *Solution selection.* The problem holder, after reflecting now on the solution suggestions, outlines what he or she proposes to do, integrating some of the feedback provided. The participants may engage in a more informal discussion again among themselves and with the problem holder, advocating for a strategy or reinforcing what the problem holder proposes to do. The problem holder may not adopt all proposed suggestions, but can state a better rationale for pro-

posed actions and anticipate better the likely consequences of the actions.

The group recommends several actions, including hosting a staff retreat to regroup and focus their work as an outgrowth of this experience, negotiating with the district office for new resources to make up for what the company had promised the community, and helping the staff and community heal from this divisive experience. The problem holder agrees that creating a staff retreat will be a useful next step to building a foundation for future work and weeding out the weak links. The group members brainstorm on how they can help facilitate the retreat—suggesting that their presence would show solidarity with and support for the staff—and identify possible inspirational speakers. The principal sketches out a new plan to get more district resources in light of the political attention the school has received.

Considering implications and actions. The final step in the discussion cycle is for the problem holder to consider how to initiate the action and policy and structural implications. The group members may brainstorm ideas of how to follow through on the proposed solution plan and anticipated organizational responses to the solution. They might help the problem holder at this stage by roleplaying conversations they might need to have with subordinates or superiors in addressing the problem.

Additional steps. Over a series of seminars, three additional discussions can be added to the collaborative inquiry discussion process, deepening the inquiry and reflection:

- Update on problems and actions taken (learning from both the negative and the positive outcomes)
- Considering relevant theory in reframing
- Reflecting on what is being learned that answers the collaborative inquiry framing question.

Over time, the initial problem-sharing activity is broadened to include updates on previously discussed problems and actions taken. This becomes an important part of the group's learning, as members learn how the proposed actions have played out and the positive and negative consequences. Sometimes, the previous problem holder uses the group-developed solutions. The group members then are eager to learn what has worked or not and in what ways. Typically, the outcomes are positive, reinforcing the group's collaborative problem-solving skills and confidence. Sometimes, the previous problem holder only uses parts of the group-developed solutions or uses his or her initial plan of action. The members of the group are very interested, in this case, to see if their cautions were on target and if the strategies have had the anticipated consequences. This consequence analysis reinforces the group's learning and perspective sharing.

> In one session, the group discusses what it gained from collaborative inquiry and how this differed from other forms of professional meeting and conversations. One principal explains that it helped him to think in broader terms and come up with strategies for his school's problems. It had allowed him to step back and see what he was not doing at the school and could. He describes it further as a reality check. Several underscore the value of being exposed to situations they might not have learned about, and learning to express what they think and feel rather than pushing feelings and experiences "down" and working in a vacuum. In between sessions, they try out things they have learned and then share the results with the group.
> ___

As the group members' collaborative problem framing and problem-solving skills deepen, they begin to see patterns among the situations and problems raised and suggest hypotheses and more generalized relationships. Some will begin to draw on readings and theoretical ideas to which they have been exposed in their preparation program experiences or other professional learning opportunities, both formal and informal.

Throughout the process and at its conclusion, the group members reflect on the meaning they are gaining in answer to the framing question of their collaborative inquiry. *What are we learning about leadership and change? What are effective approaches to leadership for school improvement?* In these reflective discussions, the participants are able to distill the lessons gained from individual problem exploration and solution discussions and examine the relationship among these and the goals as effective leaders. The facilitator can be instrumental in documenting and giving feedback from these lessons to the group for further refinement and reflection over time.

Thus, throughout, it is beneficial to reflect on the process itself and on the overarching question at the end of each session and across a few sessions. Participants gain insight into how their problem solving and collaborative learning is evolving and developing and into their accumulating understanding of the issues that frame the overarching problem as well.

SEMINAR PROCESS

Roles. There are three primary roles in the seminar itself:

- Problem holder
- Problem discussants
- Facilitator

In each seminar, one person becomes the *problem holder*, the person who is sharing a problem for group discussion, analysis, and problem solving. The other participants then become *problem discussants*, whose primary role is to help the problem holder think about his or her problem through posing probing questions, raising assumptions, reframing, and reflecting. The problem discussants may make connections to their own problems and organizational situations as well as probing for understanding and meaning.

The facilitator serves as timekeeper and provides structure, by encouraging different types of questions to deepen the discussions and problem solving. The facilitator also monitors participation, encouraging those who are too quiet to contribute and urging others who may be talking too much to make space for others. Finally, the facilitator keeps track of the threads of the discussion, the perspectives and assumptions raised, and the solutions generated. The facilitator then summarizes and shares this information at subsequent meetings to provide continuity and the learning and further reflection.

Throughout the process, all participants share the role of co-learners and co-inquirers. All take turns providing advice to others and receiving it in turn. Through reflection on discussions of past seminars, the group members can explore what they are learning, both individually and collectively.

Use of protocols. Initially, it is useful for the group to start by using a protocol to structure and guide their inquiry. The process outlined here is detailed in a protocol in Appendix A. Other useful protocols for alternative discussions can be found in McDonald, Mohr, Dichter, and McDonald's (2003) *The Power of Protocols*. This book has several useful tools for discussing aspects of work and problems. The protocol is an important learning tool for several reasons:

- It provides clear expectations for the group's work and individual roles and behavior.
- It provides time limits so that discussions do not meander away from the group's purpose and there is a clear end to the discussion.
- It makes reflection a critical part of the discussion process.
- It gives group members license to raise questions and assumptions about problems that more informal discussion convention might not allow.
- It serves as a foundation for trust building and learning.

Use of readings. While the collaborative inquiry seminar is primarily for discussions of the principals' problems and issues, there are times when readings are useful and can be introduced. The participants and facilitator will know when readings best augment or frame a discussion and which ones to suggest. Sometimes participants make connections themselves from recent articles they have read, speakers they have heard at conferences, or prior course work. Or they may ask the facilitator to make suggestions.

Matt interjects into the group discussion to describe an organizational development expert he uses in his work. "Schein," he explains (referring to Edgar Schein and his book *Organizational Culture and Change*), "gave me a way of looking at how to change difficult organizations. I used his work in my dissertation to analyze a failed school restructuring effort. It shows how important it is what a leader focuses on and what he or she models for successful change."

Time. The typical collaborative inquiry seminar takes about 90 minutes, including the initial socializing and debriefing at the end. If added into other professional development, an inquiry can be tightly conducted in 45–60 minutes, depending on how well the participants know the background of the problem holder's problem and organizational context and whether they are familiar with the protocol's pacing.

Documentation. It is important for the facilitator to keep notes on the collaborative inquiry, particularly the problem as described, the points raised by the problem discussants, how the problem was reframed, and the strategies the problem holder proposes at the end of the session. The notes become useful documentation for the group over time; they can use this to reflect on their own learning, when shared back by the facilitator in subsequent meetings.

SEMINARS OVER TIME

Cycle of problem inquiry over time. The seminars themselves follow a pattern or cycle of problem discussion over time, reflecting a deepening of the participants' needs and interests and increased facility with problem solving and reflection.

Each group is different and will vary in its capacity to learn together. We have found, however, that the cycle of collaborative inquiry over time sifts from a focus on immediate issues and problems, to an emphasis on longer-ranging, more complex problems and issues or messy organizational conditions, change, and leadership, to a convergence on appreciative inquiry.

Immediate crisis. Initially, participants bring to the group problems that they are experiencing right now, such as a staff or student crisis that had just erupted or a difficult exchange with a supervisor. The group provides critical support on the problem, but the questioning eventually leads the problem holder to look beyond the immediate problem to explore patterns of relationships with students, staff, or supervisors and for solutions that are both specific and broader.

Deeper, organizational issues. After a few rounds of inquiry, group members begin to raise problems that are broader in scope and messier, relating to organizational conditions, that are causing ongoing organizational difficulty or hindering organizational effectiveness, such as an aging, disinterested teaching staff or a poorly coordinated leadership team. The group's attention turns to exploring these issues more deeply as well, working together to combine perspectives on motivation, professional development, rewards and consequences, and aspects of organizational development.

Organizational change. Gradually the discussions on organizational issues lead to questions about initiating and facilitating organizational change: where to begin, how much to manage at once, how to leverage change through modeling and example? With this shift, the group members' own skill at thinking about organizational change deepens and they may call on one another or the facilitator to bring in relevant readings on organizational change for the group to discuss as part of their inquiry.

Adaptive leadership. Eventually discussions of organizational change evolve into discussions on adaptive leadership in general, shifting group members from looking at their changes as technical problems to understanding their leadership role as making choices in facilitating adaptive change.[2] How do they facilitate change for teachers of differing capacities for change? How do they create the conditions and support change?

Appreciative inquiry. Toward the end of the year of collaborative inquiry, the group discussions shift toward appreciative inquiry, focusing on group members' successes and the conditions that account for these.[3] What worked well? Why? Under what conditions? What helped? Principals often find that they typically focus on problems and avoiding penalties, rather than on their successes and what works well. Through appreciative inquiry, they have the opportunity to acknowledge and discuss their successes and unpack what the conditions were, what their role was, and how such success can be replicated.

Cycle of context consideration. Over time, the group shifts the scope of the problem consideration outward, taking into consideration the group members' school community, district, and larger policy and political environments. Initially, they focus narrowly within their school itself, and then on their community context. Next, the discussions shift to take into account the role and contributions of their district office, supervisors, and officials, either as dimensions of their problems, sources of support, or other considerations. Eventually, they consider the larger policy context of their work, including changing state and federal policies, directives and actions in oversight and funding. Throughout, they are reflecting on the collaborative inquiry's overarching question at several levels—from their vantage point and from increasingly distant macroperspectives—their schools and communities, their districts, and their policy context.

Cycle of career inquiry over time. The developmental cycle of focus of collaborative inquiry seminars mirrors the developmental stages of new leaders as outlined by Parkay et al. (1992) in their study of the problem solving of new principals. According to their case study research of 12 principals, principals develop through five stages: *survival, control, stability, educational leadership*, and *professional actualization.*

It is not surprising, then, that paralleling the collaborative inquiry discussions over time is a reflection on one's career future and pathways. The consideration of one's career—Should I stay or should I go? Should I seek advancement? Should I seek employment elsewhere?—is never far from the discussions of problems and challenges. The career discussions similarly shift over time from a questioning of whether one is right for the position, school, or district to eventually wondering if one is ready for advancement or more challenging conditions elsewhere.

CHAPTER 3

Collaborative Inquiry and Professional Development

The previous chapters described what we know of principals' work and the development of the Collaborative Inquiry Leadership Seminar. And while we understand some of principals' contexts and challenges, we have yet to fully understand how principals *learn* to lead. Here we continue our discussion of collaborative inquiry as professional development by pausing to explore the nature of learning and the connection to leadership development. It is because of the complex—and often unseen—relationship between learning and leading that collaborative inquiry can be most useful in both uncovering and building on that relationship. Once that relationship is uncovered, we can then identify ways in which both learning and leading can be strengthened. We address the following key ideas:

- Adult learners have specific needs and approaches that must be taken into consideration when designing professional development.
- Professional development must address the individual needs of leaders, as well as the inherently social nature of leadership.
- Professional development must incorporate a variety of learning opportunities that develop necessary thinking and leadership skills.
- Collaborative inquiry provides a structure and process that leaders can use to identify and take action on a question or problem of practice.

This chapter examines several questions central to understanding the role of professional development in learning *and* leading. The first of these is the question of what it means to learn. A related question is how to generate new ideas, new ways of thinking among leaders. This leads to the question of why collaborative inquiry is a better way of learning. And finally, there is the question of how we can develop leaders. To answer these questions it is necessary to understand adult learning and collaborative inquiry from a more theoretical-philosophical-historical perspective. This, in a way, provides a context for why, and how, collaborative inquiry is a powerful learning opportunity for school leaders.

WHAT IT MEANS TO LEARN

The idea of adult learning—as distinct from the learning of children—did not seem to matter until the late 1960s and 1970s with the work of Malcolm Knowles (1962, 1978). Previously, little thought had been given to *whether* adults learn, much less on *how* they learn. As a result, learning—or training—opportunities for adults operated from a didactic approach in which adults were passive recipients of expert, or more expert, knowledge. Some would argue that this is still the case today. Without careful attention to the process and needs of adults as learners the question of how to foster learning cannot be addressed.

The prevalent learning models of the time were based on our understanding of children's needs and the perspective of children as dependent learners. Unlike children, adults approach learning less out of pure curiosity—although that may sometimes be present—and more out of a need or with a purpose in mind. Adults, as learners, are self-directed, possess a greater quality and quantity of experience as the foundation for learning, have needs based on changing professional or personal roles, experience learning as life- and problem-centered, and are motivated by internal factors (Merriam, 2001). The differences in process and needs require the development of a new learning model—an adult learning model—that both capitalizes on and incorporates these differences.

Many adult-learning proponents (e.g., Knowles, 1978; Merriam, 2001; Mezirow, 2000) have argued that programs designed for adults must shift away from a "skill transmission" model of learning to a "competency development" model. Training and programs based on the development of competency must be more diversified and flexible, responsive to the needs of participants, more individualized, and connected to resources in the entire community. Others have emphasized the need to take into account the context of the learning and the learner, both as an individual and as a member of an organization. In other words, understand that individuals work within an organizational and cultural context that shapes both the learning and the learning experience (Grace, 1996; Lave & Wenger, 1991). This *situated learning theory* (Lave & Wenger, 1991) stresses the relationship between the learner, the activity, and the social context. This relationship must be considered when thinking about adult learners.

The focus on the characteristics of learners and those issues that influence learning are important, but this still does not get to the heart of what it means to learn. According to Mezirow (2000), adults possess "frames of references" that help them to develop attitudes toward and behaviors about the world. These frames of reference allow adults to make sense of the world and organize their experiences into a meaningful description of their lives. While these frames are important and highly personal, they are not—or should not be—rigid. Learning, therefore, occurs when adults "elaborate existing frames of reference, learn new frames of reference, transform points of view, or transform habits of mind" (p. 19). These transformations are initiated by reflecting on an experience that challenges existing frames of reference, such as an unexpected problem, a novel situation, or a new role. This kind of critical reflection, then, leads to "more dependable" frames of reference that offer a broader, or better, understanding of the situation/problem and can be applicable to other situations/problems. This process of taking frames of reference apart and building them back up again or of adding onto them is central, and unique, to adult learning.

If we apply this model of adult learning to the work of principals, it is possible to see the relationship between learning—developing new frames of reference—and leading, gaining a better understanding of a situation/problem. As principals learn they develop new frames of references for their work; new ways of understanding problems and other leadership challenges; and, ultimately, new ways of leading. This adult-learning model challenges our assumptions—or frames of reference—of principals as learners and of the way that professional development is conducted. See Figure 3.1 for some criteria for fostering adult learning.

HOW TO GENERATE NEW WAYS OF THINKING

There is relatively limited research on how to improve the way principals learn or think about their work. For some insight into how to do that, we looked at the research on teacher professional development. This research highlights some effective professional development practices that improve teachers' work. Many have stressed that these reform types of professional development—study groups,

Figure 3.1. Processes of adult learning.

Development of a climate that fosters collaboration and learning

Involvement of learners in planning

Articulation of learning needs

Formulation of learning objectives

Creation of learning plans

Implementation of learning plans

Evaluation of learning

---

mentoring, and coaching—are more responsive to teachers' needs and how they learn and are more likely to influence teacher practices (e.g., Darling-Hammond, 1997; DuFour & Eaker, 1998; Lieberman & Grolnick, 1997). Similarly, professional development activities that (1) focus on content knowledge, (2) incorporate active learning strategies, and (3) are consistent with other professional learning are more likely to improve practice in the long term (Garet, Porter, Desimone, Birman, & Yoon, 2001). Not surprisingly, learning is more meaningful if it takes place in a group setting and is sustained over time. These practices incorporate adult-learning strategies and, we argue, are likely to benefit how we design principal professional development as well.

Several active learning strategies are now widely accepted as effective for individual learning and capacity building. These include problem-based learning strategies, reflective practice, storytelling, and formation of a learning community.

Problem-based learning. As noted earlier, adults approach learning as a way of resolving a life/work–based problem. By enabling participants to "grapple with realities" (Kotinsky in Hugo, 2002) that emphasize the dynamic nature of their lives, they can make links between the professional development setting and their work. In addition, "problem based education coupled with reflection and action would allow adults consciously to exercise control over the society in which they lived" (Hugo, 2002, p. 18). The use of these problems then becomes the foundation for learning and gives rise to critical thinking and empowerment among participants (Brookfield, 1987).

Reflective practice. Schön (1987) highlights the importance of the relationship between creating a culture of reflection and fundamental change in practice. Reflection leads to the development of critical thinking, in which individuals learn to identify and challenge latent assumptions, begin to recognize the context of the problems and how these interact in a political environment, and explore alternative ways of thinking and problem solving (Brookfield, 1987).

These skills manifest themselves in the individual's engagement in deep and continuous learning. Developing reflective practitioners becomes an important element of professional development.

Storytelling/dialogue. Storytelling and narrative research (Clandinin & Connelly, 1995, 2000) show that describing a situation enables the teller to generate and examine the whole, rather than the parts. The teller is also able to relive the event, but with sufficient distance to be able to identify important details, patterns, and perspectives. Through the elaboration of a current situation, the storyteller—and the listeners—can imagine new or alternate "endings." Storytelling also allows participants to reframe an existing problem with the purpose of seeking a different solution and taking new action.

Critical questioning. Fundamental to all the strategies mentioned above is the role of questioning. Brookfield (1987) describes critical questioning as the process of discovering—or uncovering—deeply held and ingrained assumptions. These assumptions are the foundation for our frames of reference. To change our frames of reference, it is necessary to externalize the underlying assumptions. This requires a unique style of questioning. To acquire the skills to critically question, Brookfield offers some guidelines: Be specific, move from particular to general, and be conversational.

Learning communities/communities of practice. Important to learning is membership into a group of learners. Through the process of acceptance into the group—or even the development of a new group—participants learn the formal, expert knowledge of the group, as well as the expected norms and behaviors (Brown & Duguid, 1991). Learning communities shape the content, process, and conditions for their learning. In this way participants become responsible to one another for their learning. This is the foundation for learning communities.

For leaders, participating with these kinds of learning strategies provides both a foundation for further learning and models of how to engage teachers in similar professional development experiences. These are important elements of improving schools and a powerful source of motivation for principals.

WHY COLLABORATIVE INQUIRY IS A BETTER WAY OF LEARNING

Collaborative inquiry[1] integrates much of what we discussed in the previous section (adult-learning theory, effective strategies, and so on) into a formalized process of joint study. The collaborative inquiry process is based on the idea that adults can learn by directing their own research and by drawing on their lived experiences. This way of studying a problem leads to the creation of new knowledge, new courses of action, and the empowerment of participants. To understand why collaborative inquiry is a "better" way of learning, we need to know more about what it is. By exploring the process, necessary skills, and assumptions about knowledge inherent in collaborative inquiry, we can begin to see how it can provide a new way of fostering learning and professional development.

The collaborative inquiry process. Collaborative inquiry is based on several cycles of reflection and action, constructed around a shared and compelling question. Each cycle represents the movement between individuals being "researchers" of their own practice (reflection) and the "subjects" of the research (action). The essence of collaborative inquiry "is an aware and self-critical movement between experience and reflection which goes through several cycles as ideas, practice, and [in which] experiences are systematically honed and refined" (Reason, 1988, p. 6). Through this process, in which participants are both researchers and subjects, knowledge is generated from their lives and experiences. This knowledge is then developed into a working theory of their work, which is "tested" in the next cycle of action. Participants continue through these cycles until "the initial questions are fully answered in practice" (Reason, 1994, p. 44).

Collaborative inquiry skills. In addition, collaborative inquiry fosters the development of two types of skills: "informative inquiry skills and transformative inquiry skills" (Heron, 1996, p. 19). Informative inquiry skills are those that facilitate gathering information; transformative inquiry skills are those that focus on the understanding the context of the work. For Reason (1988) these skills are "in short supply in our world today" (p. 20) and adults must initiate more opportunities to collaborate in solving problems, support one another, and critically examine their world. Both informative and transformative skills are necessary in order to create a change in practice.

"Knowing" in collaborative inquiry. Critical to the development and practice of collaborative inquiry is the use of an "extended epistemology" (Reason, 1994, p. 42), which broadens our understanding of what knowledge is and how it is created. Heron (1971, 1981, 1996) outlined different kinds of knowing that define the human experience:

- *Experiential* knowledge is derived from our interactions with people, places, and things.
- *Practical* knowledge is gained from knowing how to do something through the practice of doing it.
- *Propositional* knowledge is accepted knowledge about something and the theories that are in use underlying that knowledge.
- *Presentational* knowledge is the ways in which we express or represent our understanding.

These forms of knowledge recognize the different ways in which humans understand the world. It also helps to connect that "knowledge" and the ways in which it is represented. All these are interdependent and related to our understanding of the world and who we are.

This framework provides a way of exploring the nature of learning and its relation to professional development. By providing an alternative way to view knowledge, it also provides a different way to foster learning. Professional development must address and incorporate the different "knowledges" that individuals bring with them. It requires a constructive approach to determining content and process and identifying learning. Collaborative inquiry therefore provides a different model for understanding both how we know things and how we act on what we know, especially in our practice and leadership. In the simplest terms, collaborative inquiry provides a different perspective on how we learn. It thus serves a dual purpose of (1) solving specific questions around practice and (2) engaging the learners (in this case, principals) in a process that helps them develop and exercise essential thinking, learning, and leadership skills.

HOW TO DEVELOP LEADERS AND LEADERSHIP

Much effort and thought has been invested in our understanding of leadership and leadership development in education. Leadership, as we see it, is both an individual and a communal action; it is fundamentally the relationship between leader and followers. As such, development of leaders is a process that must address leader development—the building of individual capacity—and leadership development, the social context and relationship among individuals. Leadership development, therefore, is "the expansion of a person's capacity to be effective in leadership roles and processes . . . that enable groups of people to work together in productive and meaningful ways" (McCauley et al., 1998, p. 4). This definition stresses the development of both individual capacity in a variety of leadership roles and processes and the importance of leading others and leading with others. As Wheatley (2000) stresses, personal transformation and change are at the center of effective leadership development.

Leadership development can be enhanced through three strategies—creating a variety of developmental experiences, enhancing the ability to learn from experience, and integrating various developmental experiences and embedding them in the organizational context (McCauley et al., 1998)—that enable leaders to examine existing frames of reference and develop new frames of reference or modify existing ones. The focus is on leadership as an ongoing process of evolving self-awareness, systemic thinking, and creativity.

These perspectives on leadership development highlight three important issues. The first is the tension between individual leader needs and the social context of leadership. While leadership development often focuses on the individual, it often does not prepare leaders for the social aspects of their role. Second, the idea of leadership as relational resonates with the concept of learning as a social act. Here again, the focus is on the relationship between learning and leading. Third, it reinforces the need for leadership development to address dynamics created between the individual and the collective in leadership and learning.

SUMMARY AND IMPLICATIONS

This overview highlights several important connections between adult learning, professional development, and collaborative inquiry. First, leadership development must facilitate a variety of knowledge and adult-learning needs, given principals' often novice status but varied prior experience. Second, it must be contextualized, based on the challenging conditions they are addressing and the more localized needs of the district. Third, it must foster a learning community to reduce principal isolation and strengthen commitment. Finally, and most important, it must be structured as reflective practice—both as a means and a goal—to enable problem diagnosis, exploration of complexity, management of ambiguity, and multiframed problem solving, particularly in facilitating organizational change.

Central to all professional development is individual learning, which is facilitated best by taking into account the processes of adult learning and the forms that this learning takes, the assumption being that new learning will lead to a concomitant change, and improvement, in practice. Woven throughout our discussion is our belief that how one learns is closely connected to how one leads. Conversely, how we lead is related to what we are open to learn. And while this relationship is often unconscious, through collaborative inquiry we seek to make the invisible visible as a means to foster learning and strengthen leadership. The dynamic between learning and leading is at the heart of our work and our ideas about what professional development should be.

CHAPTER 4

Developing and Managing the Inquiry

In the previous chapters we discussed principals' needs, what collaborative inquiry is, and why we think it is a useful tool for professional development. In this chapter we focus on the more "nuts and bolts" issues of how to convene and facilitate a collaborative inquiry (CI). To do this we will draw on our experience with the Collaborative Inquiry Leadership Seminar (CILS) and other inquiries in which we have been involved, in the framework of the following key ideas:

- C inquiry has four "phases": invitation, initiation, duration, and conclusion.
- Each phase requires an awareness of inherent challenges and ways of addressing them.
- The role of "convenor" evolves from bringing the collaborative inquiry together to becoming a co-inquirer.
- Relationships are key to CI.
- Ending a CI is as difficult as beginning one.

Here we outline the process of forming a CI group from beginning to end and all the murkiness in between. We have divided CI into four "phases." (Unlike the inquiry components discussed in Chapter 2 or the inquiry cycles discussed in Chapter 3, which identify what happens during a CI session, these phases represent the typical CI experience over time.) The first is the *invitation*, in which those interested are given the opportunity to learn more about CI and ask questions. The second phase is the *initiation*, when participants begin to form as a group of co-inquirers and define their question. The third is what we call the *duration*, in which participants explore their question through cycles of reflection and action. This phase lasts as long as it takes to answer the initial question to the satisfaction of all participants. The fourth phase, the *conclusion*, is when participants have decided that their question has been answered. In some cases this is also when a final "product" is created for public sharing. In a way, this chapter serves as a road map on convening and maintaining CI. It also provides a discussion of issues to be aware of, potential roadblocks, and some strategies for addressing these.

THE INVITATION

We recognize that in CI, as in life, first impressions are important. Therefore, the invitation to join is an important and first step in developing the relationships that are the foundation of CI. This initial outreach to potential participants can leave lasting impressions that either elevate or undermine the work of the group. CI is about learning together, creating new knowledge, being critical of practice in a methodical way, and improving the conditions of our work. The invitation has to reflect and reassure participants that "not knowing" is a critical part of the inquiry.

As such, careful thought must be given to how CI purpose and process and the facilitator's role are introduced to potential participants:

- Too much emphasis on the ambiguity of the process and people will not be able to connect the inquiry to their work.
- Too much focus on the outcomes will disguise the, often ambiguous, relationship between reflection and action that are at the heart of the process.
- Too much direction, and the participants will expect a facilitator-centered experience; not enough direction, and participants will wonder about your role.

The invitation occurs before the CI begins, most often at a general information session for all those interested in participating. From this session a smaller group will continue to form the CI.

It is worth thinking about the invitation as one way to demonstrate to the participants what the CI will be like. Thus, the invitation has to be open and collaborative. Equally important is who extends the invitation. The person extending the invitation must have a level of credibility among potential participants either through direct experience or through some other form of work related to their experience (i.e., research, task forces, and so on) or some other relationship (previous collaboration). Participants must be aware also of who the other participants will be, and groups should be constructed as a means of minimizing tensions and maximizing openness and trust. For the invitation to be successful, both how the invitation is extended and who extends it are important steps.

Potential roadblocks. Conveners should be aware of potential roadblock that could hinder the invitation to join the CI. These roadblocks could do much to impede the development of a collaborative inquiry.

> *Preconceived notions of professional development.* Often professional development (PD) is rarely about professional growth but instead is about compliance and skills-based training. Also, PD is usually "expert centered," relying heavily on the knowledge of consultants removed from the context of principals. As such, PD is often seen as unrelated to the real work of school leaders. Because of this previous experience with organized PD, there will be high level of skepticism around "how is this different from any other PD I've had" and "how much more work will this be."
>
> *The insider-outsider dynamic.* Another area of skepticism will be around the facilitator's role as an "outsider." In this context, *outsider* has many meanings: It can imply outside the system as we were or in the system but outside the school or principalship. Participants will be asking themselves, "What do

you want from me?" and "What can *you* do for *me*?" Because of the levels of scrutiny that principals are under, most are wary of strangers. The invitation must somehow reflect the facilitator's understanding—and respect for—this dynamic.

Established relationships. Another form of the insider-outsider dynamic can also occur among participants. Within the group there will be different kinds of relationships, from strangers to colleagues to good friends; some will feel more accepted and comfortable than others. This will be especially noticeable at the information session.

Institutional support. Ideally this kind of PD would be sanctioned by the school district. The long-term and intense nature of CI requires high levels of commitment from participants and the district. This process is one that promotes empowerment. Therefore there may be resistance at higher levels because of the loss of control over the direction the group takes. How the CI work is supported by the district over time should be addressed with the participants collectively, and revisited as needed.

What to do. The following are some strategies that may be useful in addressing the roadblocks discussed above.

Tap into a professional network. In other words, get help from an "insider." The facilitator or convener should reach out to people to help develop the CI and identify some of their colleagues who might be interested (if it is constructed on an optional basis). This will also help the facilitator to gain a better understanding of the context of the participants and avoid mistakes along the way. Keep in mind, however, that this may limit the kind of participant, so be sure to look for other places for participants.

Focus on CI as a learning experience. When introducing CI, help participants to understand that it is a tool for exploring their own practice and learning about how to improve the quality or context of their work. The questions about their work will determine the work of the CI in terms of reflection and action. Assure participants that the outcome—what was learned or improved—cannot be determined at the outset; rather, the outcome is at the heart of their questions and the decisions they make about action. As such it is at the heart of the CI.

Get to know one another. The information session or first meeting is crucial in setting the foundation for the CI. During this session the facilitator should take time to learn about participants' reasons for being there (these may be as varied as "because he told me to come" to "I've been looking for a way to work with other principals"). It is also extremely important for the facilitator to be open about him- or herself and questions about the process. This will begin to create a climate of inquiry, encourage participants to ask questions, and get skepticism out in the open.

Attention to comfort. During the information meeting—and throughout the CI—it is important that people feel valued and at ease. So pay attention to details, such as the site for the CI, room to be used, seating arrangements (round vs. square tables), timing, and lighting. Refreshments are good icebreakers, with the added benefit that eating together is an essential part of community building.

THE INITIATION

Once participants have agreed to participate in the inquiry, the first few sessions—or the "initiation" phase—are crucial for maintaining interest, firming commitment, and developing a question to focus problem sharing. In most cases participants have understood the purpose of the inquiry—to learn—and are prepared to focus on the process. This does not necessarily mean that participants are comfortable with a process-oriented method, but they are prepared to "give it a try" because of the benefits they perceive (the invitation). The initiation must also find a balance between the process and the promise of CI; in other words, attention must be given to both process *and* outcomes.

This is a critical time for the inquiry and participants. It is during the initiation that the group works on crafting their question. Once the invitation has been extended, and accepted, care must be given to understanding, addressing, and balancing individual and group needs and interests. This entails careful listening and negotiation before the final question is agreed upon. The more that participants feel that they are heard and are involved in the development of the question, the stronger the CI will become.

It is during the initiation that participants commit to the group or choose not to participate. There are several reasons for individuals to leave the inquiry, ranging from lack of interest in the question, time constraints, or lack of confidence in the process. The participant should be encouraged—not forced—to stay, especially since the group has begun to form with that participant as a member. The option of rejoining the inquiry is one that should be considered. However, once the inquiry has begun to take shape and the group has been solidified, it is difficult to incorporate a "new" member. The loss of any member, even at this early stage, is difficult, and the remaining participants should be given the opportunity to discuss it if necessary.

The initiation is complex phase in which both the inquiry and the group are vulnerable. Despite any difficulties, remaining members will be firmly committed to the question, the inquiry, and one another.

Potential roadblocks. As in the invitation, those interested in starting a CI will encounter some stumbling blocks during the initiation phase as well.

> *Posturing.* As new principals, participants may feel the need to "convince" their peers about their ability to do their job. This sometimes takes the form of simple "showing off" or "talking big" to one another. The belief among many at the beginning is that any sign of uncertainty or ignorance will be perceived as weakness and poor leadership. While this is

an important part of the process of getting to know one another, if it lasts too long, participants will grow bored and disillusioned with the inquiry.

Range of leadership experience. Even though participants may have the same number of years in the principalship, they will have a range of leadership experience in schools (as teachers, assistant principals, union reps, and so on). Similarly in their personal lives they may have exercised leadership in other contexts (e.g., churches, community organizations). Depending on these, what they want from the CI will also range from basic skills/survival to more complex understandings of their leadership. Equally important, for some their goals for the CI may be separate from their career goals, whereas for others they will be linked.

Lack of leadership awareness. Part of the process of formulating a question is dependent upon participants having an understanding of their leadership needs, goals, and strengths and weaknesses (not to be confused with "administrative" issues such as time management). This helps the group to understand where their leadership "edges" lie and to develop an appropriate question. Another part of the process is participants realizing that they often "don't know what they don't know." Formulating a question to which they already know the answer is not suitable for a CI. When participants do not have this level of *leadership awareness* it can prolong the initiation phase and constrain the development of the group.

Search for affirmation. Early on, participants may see the CI as a chance to affirm their leadership decisions, instead of problem exploration and question posing (the real intent of CI). As a result, participants may pose problems or issues that they do not really want to understand or reframe; rather, they want others to agree to the action(s) taken. When the CI process begins, therefore, they may feel defensive and see the group's questioning as undermining their leadership competence. This can stifle the discussion of the prob-

lem and limit involvement. It also can signal that participants have yet to understand the purpose of CI. The facilitator can pause the discussion to revisit the purpose of the
discussion and questions.

Focus on problem-solving skills. Participants may interpret the CI
to be *only* about developing problem-solving skills, search-
ing for the one "right way" to do it. Problem solving, by
itself, is bounded by time and issue and, as a skill, has limited
long-term impact on leadership development. In many
respects problem solving requires leaders to recognize a
problem and then apply a strategy that previously had been
successful in a similar situation. This strategy may work in
many instances, but in others it can aggravate an existing
issue. Complexities and subtle differences become apparent only after a given strategy has failed. While problem
solving is an important leadership skill, in CI it is embedded in the larger context of question posing and leadership
development. In essence, what does the participant want
to learn about their leadership before, during, and after the
problem has occurred? If participants overlook how the
inquiry in *collaborative inquiry* is an essential element of
the group process, then the CI will have limited success in
developing their leadership.

What to do. These roadblocks can be overcome by using some of
the following strategies, which we found have helped us during the
initiation phase:

Develop learning norms. To develop learning norms and guidelines for individual and group behavior, participants must
be able to articulate individually what helps them to learn.
This is more than simply "turn off cell phones during sessions." It means knowing the behaviors, your own and those
of others, that help you learn. It can include "being able to
say stop or call a break" during a discussion when feeling
overwhelmed or "time to think/write before beginning the

discussion" for those who need to process in order to focus or "tell the group when you've checked out" so that the person has the opportunity to reengage with the group. Again the emphasis is on what helps individuals learn so that the group can learn and work together. It also helps to refocus individual "posturing" to group needs. Additionally, it helps to strengthen the CI as a learning process.

Develop questions. As obvious as it sounds, one of the most important things to do is to focus the initiation on finding a question. To do this, the group must listen to—and accept—differences in motivations, goals, and issues. Among these differences, the participants need to look for similarities and find areas of common interest. This will point to a question or even a series of questions. There will be a gravitational pull to find the "right" question so that the group can get started and the "work" can begin. This pull must be resisted. The question will develop naturally through discussion, sharing, and reflection (here again, preparing participants for cycles of action and reflection). Ultimately, the group will believe that the question will emerge if the conveners and facilitators believe it.

Make time to take time. The first real challenge that emerges in CI is the issue of time. As in the development of the question, participants will want to define it as soon as possible, even if prematurely. Similarly, the necessary time must be given to continuing relationship building as a way to strengthen the group and the inquiry (countering the assumption that because the group "gets along" it is ready to study its practice together). For principals this is a difficult task, given their multiple demands. But for this same reason, it is extremely important that the CI be a "timeless" place where the focus is on *quality* of thought and process, rather than *quantity*. The group must come to understand that time does not need to be broken down into smaller segments in order to be used efficiently or effectively. Rather, by creating a common, collaborative space where time is redefined, the group is allowed to focus on the more important issue of its learning.

THE DURATION

The duration covers the bulk of the CI experience, during which most of the work takes place over time. As participants evolve into deeper and more sustained inquiry, new challenges and issues arise. Just as in the invitation and initiation process, care must be given to how the CI evolves and the changing needs of the group. The duration phase is where the ongoing work and motivation of the group must be maintained and reinforced when necessary.

By now participants have a better understanding of CI, how it will help their leadership, and what their question is. The challenge now becomes implementing ongoing cycles of action and reflection. This raises new challenges for the group and the facilitator (at this phase the role of the convener is ended and, depending on the circumstances, he or she becomes either a co-inquirer or a facilitator). Issues that may have seemed resolved or unrelated before begin to make more of an impact on the inquiry.

It is necessary here to take a moment to explain the cycles of action and reflection. There is no "right" way of conducting a CI other than engaging in these cycles in a collaborative, methodical, and democratic manner. While we have outlined in Chapter 2 a recommended set of steps for conducting CI, the group can decide on what kinds of actions and reflections to engage in, how often, to what end, and how to work together. There is no blueprint for a "good" CI; the group works to develop an inquiry that meets its needs and answers its question, as guided by its core principles. This is not to say that this is a random process of hit-or-miss. Participants have agreed to study their own leadership and as such need to develop a rigorous inquiry discussion and problem solving process.

The duration phase may last anywhere from a few weeks to months to years, again, depending upon the question and the group. Sustaining interest and energy throughout are important in seeing the inquiry to its natural conclusion.

Potential roadblocks. Here some of the roadblocks that appeared previously resurface as participants begin to understand and take ownership of their collaborative inquiry seminars. It is during the cycles of action reflection that many of the leadership, learning, and communication differences among participants emerge. These appear in some of the following ways.

> *Misuse of storytelling.* Participants often share their experiences through stories. Two kinds of stories can take over the inquiry. The first is "war stories." While these often create camaraderie, they are often a retelling of events with little emphasis on understanding or reframing the experience, much less on finding a solution. They typically have complex details and tangents, with the teller serving as hero or victim at the story's center. Another kind of story is group venting or "chasing their tales." Here the group jointly tells a story of an experience they can all relate to (usually about the district office). By doing so they reinforce their perspectives, but fail to look critically at the situation or their actions. Neither of these forms of storytelling, while entertaining, contribute to learning. It is the facilitator's responsibility to limit these kinds of problem identification and guide the group to engage in critical analysis and reflection.
>
> *Weak reflection skills.* Reflection is a skill that is little understood and, in the context of daily school leadership demands, little used or appreciated. It is not surprising, then, that participants are not sure how to be reflective. Participants often respond in one of two ways, when asked to be reflective about a problem or situation. One is to project their experience or feelings onto another's problem. For example, when discussing a union issue, participants would share what

they did or how they felt but not think about why they did that or if the outcomes were actually positive. The other is by reflecting at a superficial level, as though skipping stones on water. In the same example, participants focus on one incident and share their actions, but do not consider long-term patterns or consequences that could indicate a deeper problem. Without the development of necessary reflection skills, learning is limited.

Misguided "help." Above all, participants want to be helpful, and by doing so, they may short-change inquiry and problem solving. They often do this in two ways. The first is by "playing nice" and not bringing a critical perspective to the group for fear of being insulting or hurting someone's feelings. Another way is by providing advice rather than contributing to the inquiry. Advice can be either misdirected or unwanted, particularly when offered early in the inquiry process. If we follow the example of union trouble, participants may give advice on how to reassign the union rep when the problem may be something different, thereby misdirecting the participant. Unwanted advice occurs when the group responds before the participant is ready to "hear" any alternate solutions, causing the participant to become defensive and short-changing the analysis and solution generation.

Resistance. Despite their commitment to the CI, some participants may continue to resist engaging thoughtfully in the process, particularly in addressing their own problems or issues. One clear form of expressing resistance is through absenteeism and lack of participation when present. This is different from lack of interest, in that the participant does want to engage in the inquiry, yet finds ways of limiting involvement, often citing work-related stress and demands that serve as distractions. Another, often unconscious, form is to raise walls and use defense mechanisms that inhibit learning. This is particularly true for participants who insist on personalizing their problems, turning any attempt to reframe or find solutions into a personal attack. These forms of resistance will seriously limit individual learning, and they require skillful facilitation to shift the inquiry to the resistant behavior.

Becoming facilitator dependent. In instances of uncertainty, the group will look to the facilitator to provide leadership and direction. It is easy to let the facilitator make decisions and focus the group when necessary. While this is initially helpful, the participants must gain these skills themselves; at its heart, CI is a democratic process. If the group allows itself to rely on the facilitator, then power can shift too much toward the facilitator, bringing into question who the CI is for.

What to do. The following ideas were helpful in addressing the roadblocks and in smoothing some of the challenges inherent in CI.

Frame differences as strengths. We have discussed in several places the importance of recognizing individual differences and of paying attention to these in relation to the group and the CI. In reality many of the roadblocks discussed stem from individual differences and differences in expectations/goals. It is one thing to be aware of these and another to know what to do with them. Rather than gloss over differences, CI allows participants to see them as valuable learning tools. Differences allow others to understand problems in new ways, to see the individuals involved in a new light, to develop new solutions, and to improve leadership skills. While initially irritating, differences must be allowed to surface as a strength of the group.

Develop a process and language. The sooner the group develops a process for organizing and engaging in the CI, the better, and developing a process is critical learning for the group. The process that was developed for our CI, as outlined in Chapter 2, emerged through group discussions about how to improve problem solving in the inquiry process. Adopting a structured protocol process gave the group a shared process language and a means of monitoring its own work, such as in better recognizing when group members were off topic or had moved from reflection to action prematurely. This also allowed the group to be less dependent on the facilitators.

Connect group learning and individual practice. The more that participants see the connection between group learning and their own practice, the more they will be able to overcome their need to dominate discussion or be resistant. One key moment for this group was the introduction of theory to the discussion. Several of the participants wanted to "know more" about an element of their leadership and looked to more theoretical constructs for better understanding. The theory was used as a guide to deepen their reflection and to pose other explanations for their practice related to this new understanding. It also allowed them to develop theory from their work. This offered a way to see theory from a new perspective. For the group, it was a clear connection between the CI and their leadership.

THE CONCLUSION

Endings are often as important as beginnings. And the quality of the ending is indicative of the quality of the CI. As such, thought must be given to how to end the CI and, more important, how to know when the CI is at an end.

Throughout the CI, the group has been investigating a question or series of questions. Their time has been spent on finding answers through cycles of action and reflection at both an individual and a group level. Chances are their question has changed slightly over time and that they have found several answers along the way that have led to better, more focused questions. Finally, they have come to rely on one another as co-inquirers and colleagues. Ending a CI, therefore, is difficult. And as much as participants may wish it to, it cannot last indefinitely.

Central to knowing when to end is knowing when questions have been answered to the satisfaction of participants. This, of course, will vary among participants (and even among CIs). One way of addressing this issue is asking at the *beginning*, "When will we know it's over?" While this seems counterintuitive, especially since participants may not be familiar with CI, it is helpful nonetheless. Any deadline set at the beginning is fluid, of course, and serves best as a guideline for knowing when the end is approaching. If at the outset participants have articulated what they need to be able to do to have "closure," the ending can include those important elements and ease the transition out of CI.

Potential roadblocks. The end, however, is not without its share of obstacles. After a fairly intense process and commitment, participants are often reluctant to "let go." This reluctance manifests itself in several ways.

> *Confusion around the answer.* Participants have been focusing so much—and for so long—on researching their practice and distilling their learning that often the "answer" to the question is taken for granted or even is anticlimactic. For some it becomes more an issue that the answer cannot be *that* (e.g., simple, unexpected). For others their individual practice may have already evolved beyond the original question, leading to other questions. Until participants can articulate the answer—or answers—to their question, they will never feel that the CI is over.
>
> *Unfinished leadership.* Some participants may feel that because some of their individual leadership questions or issues are unresolved, the original question has not been answered to their satisfaction. The focus of the CI shared here was on improving leadership, more than addressing individual leadership problems (although that was the vehicle for action and reflection). Participants who have focused more on the problem-solving focus of the CI, and less on the scope

of their leadership, may find it more difficult to know when the inquiry has ended.

CI dependence. As mentioned earlier, participants have invested a significant amount of time and energy in the inquiry. They have carved time out of their daily schedules to reflect and act; they have made it a priority to attend sessions; they have built a place where they can critically look at practice; they have become reflective practitioners. Finally, they have created a learning community. Some will feel that they cannot continue working as a learning community without the CI, regardless of whether their question has been answered. In other words they have mistaken what they have created *through* the CI as *the* CI. Until they can disentangle the two, they will not believe that the CI is done.

Who "owns" the knowledge? As the answer(s) becomes clearer, participants may wonder who actually determined what was learned along the way. Similarly, who, then, owns the knowledge? This may not be apparent immediately, but it is related to insider-outsider dynamics early in the CI. As outsiders, we learned tremendous amounts about the role of the principalship and the uses of CI. We are prepared to share this with others in the field. What role do participants play in determining what is shared and how to share it? And if they do not play a role, how can they be sure that the intent of the CI was not to do research *on* them? These are serious questions that can influence the way in which the CI ends.

What to do.

Accept that some questions/issues will be unresolved. From the beginning it is important to realize that the question developed by the group is the focus of the CI. It is up to participants—with the help of the group—to discern how their personal interests are connected to the larger question. As a result participants must realize that not all their problems will be resolved through the inquiry. Rather, the CI will address the underlying leadership issues that can be at the heart of a range of problems. Once these have been reflected and acted upon (through the cycles of the CI), participants must apply this learning to other current and potential challenges. This will help participants understand, apply, and end the CI.

Evaluate the process. One clear way to help participants end the CI experience is to turn their critical, reflective skills on the CI itself. By evaluating the process, participants can address any remaining questions about CI, the group process, or their leadership. In addition, it allows them to discuss other potential applications of their work. Finally, it helps participants clarify the answer(s) to their original leadership question. For fruitful evaluation questions, see Figure 4.1.

Make plans for post-CI. Another way to help participants see beyond the CI is through plans to make the learning public. This can be done in various ways. The most obvious can be through the publication of a joint written product. This article can be written for an academic or practitioner-based audience, depending on its purpose.

Creating a new CI opportunity. Other new CI opportunities can be explored as well, either externally with other principals

Figure 4.1. Example of evaluation questions.

Did the CI meet your expectations? How?

How were your goals met?

How did the CI change over time?

What is the relationship between action/reflection in CI?

What is the relationship between action/reflection in your practice?

How could the CI be improved?

or internally as professional development for staff. In this way participants formalize their learning and look for ways to deepen their understanding. The key is the sharing of knowledge gained through the CI.

Trust the relationships. One final consideration when ending a CI is the quality of the relationships developed. CI is an intense experience that engages participants in an exploration of their most pressing questions. Relationships are important to a strong CI and are strengthened through the CI. Participants invest and rely on these relationships. At the same time, participants must trust that these relationships will continue after the CI as long as they continue investing in one another. These relationships will bolster participants as they let go of the CI.

SUMMARY AND IMPLICATIONS

This chapter has focused on some of the pitfalls inherent in CI and how to prepare for them. This was by no means an exhaustive list and as others convene a CI, roadblocks may appear that we did not encounter. What is important to realize is that there is no cookie-cutter approach to preparing for or conducting a CI. Rather, the emphasis must be on the needs and questions of the people involved. An honest and open approach to this will do much to overcome many of these roadblocks.

The roadblocks discussed here are, in a sense, developmental as well. At each phase of the inquiry, differences will emerge in participants' understanding of the process, problems, or leadership. These will arise out of differences in experiences, learning and communication styles, needs, and perceptions. As participants meet each cycle of action reflection and learn from it, they will be faced with new understandings of themselves and their leadership. This will lead to a new "cycle" of questions about the CI and roadblocks. In any instance of professional development, therefore, it is necessary to be aware of the relationship between personal and professional identities. To focus on one at the expense of the other will create tension, both within individuals and between them. To ignore the relationship can seriously undermine any long-term learning or leadership development. Understanding this relationship is key to understanding many of the roadblocks participants pose and of finding ways to overcome them collaboratively.

CI is an extremely powerful professional development tool. The experience will shape, in many ways, how participants define themselves and their leadership. This in turn will shape where their individual inquiries will go next in terms of leadership development and practice. The CI has also provided participants with a process and tools for reflection, questioning, problem solving, and learning. These are skills and dispositions that will last beyond the inquiry because they are linked to participants' developing sense as leaders. Ultimately, this will affect how—and where—they lead their schools.

CHAPTER 5

The Facilitator/
Co-inquirer Role

This chapter is about the facilitator. In any professional development setting the facilitator plays a critical role in structuring the learning and facilitating the behavior and learning of participants. Within collaborative inquiry (CI), the role is even more important and, perhaps, more difficult. Rather than following a predetermined script the facilitator must be able to recognize and adapt to emerging questions and changing needs. This requires a different kind of facilitation from what is expected in more conventional professional development.

Facilitation often begins with understanding the purpose of an activity, determining outcomes, and creating a process that will ensure that both the purpose and outcomes are met. Because CI is not linear, the facilitation must be flexible, supportive, and often spontaneous. At the same time it must be focused, challenging, and collaborative. Even more important, the facilitator's role must *transcend* the group's process, to allow engagement as a co-inquirer in the work. Within CI, facilitation for the sake of facilitation is neither helpful nor desired. The strength of facilitators is not just in their skills of facilitation, but also in their dual role as co-inquirer. Here we will discuss the role of the facilitator and how, if navigated carefully, it can evolve into that of a co-inquirer. We explore the following key ideas:

- Facilitators must understand the philosophical *traditions* of CI.
- The role of the facilitator is threefold: structure the CI, foster participation, and focus on learning.
- An important part of the role is to model the necessary skills and dispositions.
- The needs of the group should determine the decision to facilitate or co-facilitate as well as when to take on the role of co-inquirer.
- Tension can arise around the duality of the facilitator/co-inquirer role.

This chapter includes a brief reminder of some of the foundations of CI. Next is a discussion of the role of the facilitator, followed by some ways to facilitate. For the purposes of this discussion we have tried to separate out how to facilitate the more logistical elements of facilitation (such as the structure) from the more abstract elements (such as participation and learning).

THINGS TO KEEP IN MIND

There are several things that facilitators in particular need to be aware of throughout the CI process:

- *CI is about people.* Participants bring with them professional and personal histories. In addition they may have different goals and ideas about outcomes. These must be taken into account and respected. Participants need to be given the chance to see the relationship between their professional needs, personal lives, and the CI.
- *CI is about questions.* Based on their total life experiences, participants will bring a range of questions, issues, and goals to the discussions. If they are attracted to a CI, chances are they have a high level of curiosity—especially around their roles.

The more that participants' questions can be tapped into and discussed throughout, the more they can develop their skills of reflection in action.

- *CI is about empowerment.* Key to CI is the understanding that within the group, no one person—or role—has more importance. All must be involved in developing the purpose and process of the inquiry. Initially, for example, there are different levels of knowledge about CI. More often, the conveners will know the most. Other participants will know less and some will know nothing. The imbalance created must be recognized and addressed. Information about CI must be shared in as many ways as possible in order to keep the group balanced.
- *CI is about reflection.* Reflection in CI serves several purposes. The first is to offer a structured way for participants to analyze their experiences. The second is to strengthen the group as participants engage in *joint* analysis of their leadership challenges. The third is to learn from their—and others'—experiences. Participants—and facilitators—must come to see reflection as a form of *action*. As such, time must be dedicated to enhance their reflection skills and to exercise it within the CI.
- *CI is work.* The kind of work or its purpose is not known at the beginning of the CI; but it is work nonetheless, and for some it is difficult. To engage effectively in CI, participants must be willing to suspend an orientation toward quick solutions and immediate action and replace them with in-depth exploration and deliberate action. This is something that, given the current climate, is counterintuitive, and participants must be able to resist these pressures to seek "easy" answers.

These issues must be kept in mind throughout any CI. They pose different kinds of challenges for facilitators and participants and if not shared or addressed could become the basis of the roadblocks discussed in the previous chapter. Finally, these should also be used as touchstones for any inquiry as reminders of the collaborative and democratic process embedded in CI.

THE ROLE OF THE FACILITATOR

As mentioned above, the facilitator role is complex and constantly changing. Part of the challenge—and success—of the facilitator is to enable the participants to guide the inquiry. The other part of the challenge is to, in effect, relinquish the role of facilitation and engage with the group as a co-inquirer. Through our experience as facilitators we came to understand our role as facilitators/co-inquirers, as well as certain skills and attitudes that helped us in this emerging role.

In CI, a facilitator must recognize the dual—and sometimes contradictory—need to make participants both *independent* and *interdependent* inquirers. Independent in that rather than looking to the facilitator to make sense of their experiences, articulate their learning, and make connections, they do these things for themselves. Interdependent in that the relationships fostered allow participants to draw out and draw on one another's experiences. Ideally, this interdependence can extend beyond the CI to professional relationships among participants. In moving the focus of the learning away from the facilitator and to one another, all participants become responsible for their learning, that is, independent, and that of the others, interdependent. Once this independence and interdependence are established, the facilitator has a greater opportunity to become a co-inquirer. If not, the group becomes facilitator dependent and will not develop the critical skills to wholly engage in the inquiry.

Equally important, the facilitator has to be prepared to model certain skills, both *informative* and *transformative* (Heron, 1996), which are central to the inquiry. Necessary informative skills include listening, question posing, and observation. Transformative skills include critical thinking, reflection, self-awareness, and suspension of judgment. The facilitator must also model certain dispositions that are fundamental to CI. Some basic dispositions are open-mindedness, a learning mode, empathy, and commitment. These skills and dispositions must be modeled in all interactions with participants. This modeling is important, especially at the invitation-initiation phase when participants are scrutinizing the behavior of the facilitator as they decide to participate. As the CI takes shape, the facilitator must continue to model these skills *and* the cycles of action reflection in their interactions with the group.

Perhaps most important of all, facilitators must see themselves as co-learners. CI is based on the idea that knowledge is co-constructed through joint reflection on experiences, meaning that no single participant "knows" everything. The facilitator must see her- or himself as part of the question exploration. Initially, facilitators need to actively create the conditions that allow participants to engage in CI. Ideally, as the group evolves, the facilitator takes less of a direct role as the participants "take over" the inquiry and shape it to suit their needs. As participants grow in confidence they will begin facilitating themselves. When this occurs, a facilitator knows that she or he has done a good job and is sharing the facilitation with others in the group.

All this does not mean that the role of the facilitator is not integral to CI. There will be times when the group will need grounding or guidance, usually at stages of transition (i.e., initiation, ending) or at the end of cycles of action reflection, and times when facilitation is key. Facilitator roles are outlined in Figure 5.1.

FACILITATORS OR CO-FACILITATORS

This seems an appropriate place to talk briefly about the decision to facilitate or co-facilitate. Co-facilitation is defined here as having two or more facilitators working with a group. Our experience, shared in this book, was as co-facilitators. We found this to be an enriching and powerful experience. And in many respects we see co-facilitation as the ideal situation, for several reasons.

First of all, facilitating an inquiry is difficult and draining work. CI facilitation requires a level of awareness and skill that is difficult to maintain during a given session, and even more so over time. Co-facilitation allows for each facilitator to take "breaks" or collect her or his thoughts or listen in a more focused way. Each co-facilitator can take turns being more active, while the other can step back,

Figure 5.1. Facilitator roles.

The Facilitator IS:	The Facilitator ISN'T:
• A co-inquirer	• A know-it-all
• A learner	• A consultant
• A model	• A teacher
• A question-poser	• A problem-solver
• Reflective	• Self-centered
• Supportive	• In control
• Focused on relationships	• Focused on minutiae
• Big picture-oriented	

figuratively, to observe and learn about the group. This requires that facilitators know and understand each other enough that they know when to help each other, step in, make observations, and deepen reflection. By "taking turns," co-facilitators can keep from burning out during the CI.

In addition, it is an example of two brains being better than one. By combining individual skills into one role, the role is strengthened. It is also offers facilitators the chance to improve their practice by seeing another style of facilitation and by having someone with whom to discuss facilitation in general. Similarly, co-facilitation allows for greater recall and deeper reflection on the CI. By having another facilitator who was "there" helps to refine/reframe the experience and leads to greater learning.

Last, and more important, co-facilitation models for participants (1) how differences can be strengths and (2) the importance of relationships. It was our experience that there were some fundamental similarities in our approach to facilitation and understanding of CI. Yet there were some differences in our learning and communication styles. These differences, we found, helped us to understand how the participants might experience differences. We were also able to turn to each other at different moments during the CI when one of us was having trouble understanding what was happening. The facilitation also rested on our ability to connect with individual participants. Our "differences" as facilitators let participants connect with us in different ways at varied times, which helped their learning. By seeing how we as facilitators built a relationship that allowed us to capitalize on our similarities *and* differences, participants were able to observe how we learned from and relied on each other throughout.

This is not to say that in the absence of two facilitators a CI cannot or should not be conducted. Rather, it is to emphasize that if the opportunity to co-facilitate presents itself, it should be seriously considered. Co-facilitation poses the same challenge whether it is developing a relationship with a new colleague or by working differently with a trusted colleague. And yet the learning and benefits far outweigh any obstacles.

FACILITATING THE STRUCTURE OF CI

In Chapter 2, we discussed the process of CI. That clarifies how to create a working and learning environment. Here we extend the discussion of process to address the role of the facilitator in creating that space. There are several elements of the CI that facilitators must learn to manage and, as they become accepted practice in the group, let go. It is important to note that facilitating the *structure* of the CI is necessary, but not sufficient, for an effective CI. A facilitator's energy must be directed at facilitating participation and learning—the more difficult aspects of the role—in addition to the structural needs of the group.

Logistics manager. Comfort, both emotional and physical, is important in learning and making participants feel valued. Part of the role of the facilitator, then, is to organize the logistical issues in bringing the group together. This includes things such as scheduling, location, communication, and timekeeping. This role is important for two reasons. For us, the first was that, given participants' schedules and demands, it was easier for all. The second was that we felt that the less participants had to deal with these details, the more they would be able to participate in the inquiry. It is important to recognize that some facilitators can fall into the trap of being logistics manager out of a need to control the group. Understanding the motivation to be the logistics manager is an important element of this. Since, as we have discussed often, *all* participants are empowered, the issue of control needs to be recognized and resolved immediately.

Session manager. While logistical issues need to be managed at a macro level, other issues need to be handled at a micro level within each session. This means simply starting, guiding, and ending sessions. Early on it was necessary to remind participants of the group process, especially as it was being developed from one session to the next. During the sessions it sometimes became necessary to remind participants of the process or where they were in it as a way of guiding the discussion. As questioning skills are being developed, it falls to the facilitator to foster appropriate listening and questioning strategies (with humor, of course). More often than not, the facilitator will need to help the participants to keep the process moving and to bring discussions to a close. It is essential that time be allotted at the end of each session to focus on individual application of the discussion as a way to ensure the continuing cycle of action reflection. Pacing the CI and drawing it to a close is critical for the facilitator, to keep it moving for all participants and making it easy to stop, even when discussions are engaging.

Data manager. At the heart of any CI process are cycles of action and reflection. In this CI we engaged in "action" between meetings and used the sessions for "reflection" and to pull out important insights and learning "reflection as action." It is these cycles between action and reflection that must be documented and "data" collected on problems raised, analysis and problem framing/solving, and actions to be taken. An important role, then, is managing this data as they accumulate. This includes taking notes, keeping track of participants' products (such as writing samples and artifacts), and recording/transcribing meetings. These data should be used to document the work, as tools for reflection, and to help the group formalize their learning. Participants must have access to the data and be able to determine, and comment on, their use in and outside the CI.

FACILITATING PARTICIPATION

Members of a CI often have different levels of participation and influence. The facilitator must work to engage everybody in the inquiry so that the question can be answered to the satisfaction of all the participants. Participation in CI is not limited to attendance, but rather, encompasses involvement during (reflection) and in between (action) sessions. The facilitator has to then make sure that participants have what they need to fully engage in the inquiry.

Forming an inquiry group. An important role of the facilitator is to make sure that the participants understand CI. This is more than understanding the cycles of action reflection and researching a leadership question or exploring a leadership problem—although this is important. It also means understanding the fundamental beliefs of CI: the co-construction of knowledge, the degree of empowerment, and the collaborative nature of the inquiry. Sharing of information, thinking, and expectations is one way of addressing different levels of understanding. Discussions guided by the facilitator help participants develop necessary understanding and skills.

Question development. Another role of the facilitator is to build on individual interests to develop the group's question. The facilitator's role is to help the group explore larger shared issues in which individual questions might be situated. The process of developing the question (outlined in Figure 5.2) is a learning process in and of itself. It is a way to surface and connect each participant's interests, needs,

Figure 5.2. Question development.

Individual Questions	Group Question(s)
How do I do my job better?	What is the nature of effective leadership?
How do I work with the district?	
How can I manage multiple demands?	How do effective leaders mediate the external environment?
How do I focus on instruction?	How does a principal learn this kind of leadership?
How do I protect my school?	
How do I get more for my school?	
Where do I go for help?	

and goals. The process, therefore, can be messy as participants articulate their own question(s) and try to make connections with the group.

The facilitator both draws out questions from participants and helps them see how these questions are related to one another. Embedded in the larger question are the answers to the individual questions. Confining the focus to individual questions would narrow the inquiry and limit the learning. When discussing the broader question, the facilitator must help participants to "see" their questions in the inquiry and reinforce the value of their participation.

Kinds of participation. Quality of participation is extremely important, both for the inquiry and for individual learning. With their experiences and styles, participants will engage in different ways and have different needs. In the course of this CI, we found different "types" of engagement (see Table 5.1). While these types are not exhaustive, they are illustrative of how individual learning styles can influence a collaborative inquiry. These different types are not necessarily fixed and the facilitator can help participants learn about themselves. In addition, these types can also be instrumental in how members learn about working together in a new way.

Table 5.1. Types of engagement

Typology	Behaviors	Problem
The Catalyst	Has personal magnetism and loads of charisma; often well-respected and recognized as a successful leader; usually at the forefront of new ideas and has a tendency to attract others.	The problem for the Catalyst is often unconscious; others look to him or her to lead the group (both in thinking and in action); in CI leadership needs to be shared and participation should be complete.
The Dominator	Talks too much; tells elaborate stories that seem to have multiple purposes; connects others' issues to own story; often confuses the listener.	Relives experiences rather than reflecting on them; focuses on minute details rather than larger concepts/issues; looking for affirmation of own perspective.
Reserved	Talks too little; rarely shares; uses a wide brush to relate events; treats all events as equally important.	Distances him- or herself from experiences; focuses on chronology of events rather than larger concepts/ issues; group doesn't know where to focus.
Occasional	Attendance and participation are unreliable; when does attend, time is spent bringing him or her up to date and trying to include him or her in the process.	Participation is seen as a vehicle for own agenda; contributions are viewed with suspicion; is mistrusted by the group.
The Skeptic	Limits own participation; observes others for clues on how to act; impatient with process; is cynical about potential for benefits.	Does not engage fully in his or her own or others' learning; waiting for some "sign" to know when to believe.

The role of the facilitator with these typologies, then, is to help participants recognize them and begin to develop new ways of listening, reflecting, and acting. These new skills will facilitate participant learning and are applicable to their own interpersonal relations elsewhere. The behavior(s) can be drawn upon to facilitate a new way of looking at a problem—such as the skepticism and observations of those who only participate occasionally.

FACILITATING LEARNING

Facilitating the structure of CI and the participation of members is a means of preparing for the more in-depth work of the inquiry and the learning of participants. As mentioned previously, this work cannot begin without structure and participation, and yet the facilitator can find that they are consumed by structural issues or ensuring equal participation at the expense of facilitating learning. Facilitating learning can be the most difficult and complex of all the aspects of facilitation, yet it is at the heart of the CI and the reason the group comes together. It is also the reason *for* facilitating. If participants are not learning, the quality of the structure or the participation really does not matter. The facilitator must focus on what is helpful to participant learning.

Strategies for questioning. One of the most important roles a facilitator can play is that of posing questions. Questions are a tool for information gathering, theory testing, predicting, and reflection. Questions are very important in CI. As noted in Chapter 2, we came to rely on protocols to guide the questioning, particularly early on, when those skills were being developed. By providing a framework for appropriate questions and for question forming, protocols are an important learning tool. Another strategy that we incorporated into our CI was the analysis of mental models. By making participants bring their thinking to the group—out loud—we were able to uncover patterns in thinking as well as errors in logic. The analysis of these mental models led to powerful breakthroughs for some and important learning for all. In terms of questioning, it is also important for facilitators to help participants reflect on their defense mechanisms in use (both in the CI and in their practice) and to challenge "group think," which can endanger the learning of any group.

Formalizing reflection. As we mentioned in Chapter 4, reflection is a skill that participants often need help to develop as a habit of practice. Questions, by their very nature, foster reflection. There are other useful means of formalizing reflection, both as a process and as a product. One way is to capture individual and group stories through writing, drawing, and other artifacts of their work. Another is to identify metaphors that illustrate what participants think about their leadership. By having participants uncover the assumptions hidden in their metaphor, they gain a deeper understanding of how they see leadership, generally, and how they perceive their leadership, specifically.

The CI also provides a stable environment and sustained feedback on participants' actions, thinking, and leadership. Part of the role of the facilitator is to keep track of all this to provide a running record of the group's process, work, and outcomes. (The kind of "data" that can be collected was discussed previously.) This process formalizes reflection as a critical part of participants' learning.

Validating learning. Formalizing many of the tools for questioning, action, and reflection serves another purpose, that of validating learning. Knowing that learning is a developmental process, participants need to be able to identify their growth over time. Equally important, group members must be able to identify their learning, to articulate it, to "name" it, meaning that participants must be able to state, "I started at point A and now I'm at point C." Equally important, they must be able to say, "And this is *why* I moved from A to C and I know I still need to get to point D." It is this identification and articulation of what they have learned, how they have developed, and why it is important to their leadership that makes this aspect of facilitation so important to the CI.

Another way of doing that is through the "action" of problem framing/solving and giving feedback to other participants. These "actions" allow them to apply, in an immediate way, what they have learned. By bringing attention to how this has evolved over time allows participants to realize how much they have learned and changed. Learning is validated over time as participants witness the outcomes of what each did as a consequence of the group discussions of their problem or issue. This feedback enables each participant to learn—and to discuss as a group—whether their predictions and recommendations for a situation or issue bear out. Linking the results back to their original analyses helps the group members make connections and reinforces their new problem-solving frames.

EVALUATING THE INQUIRY

To ensure that the CI is meeting participants' needs, there must be a system for constant feedback and improvement. It is important to note here that the evaluation mechanisms are less for the facilitator—although it is necessary—and more for the participants themselves to determine how the CI is answering their question(s). In the event that participants determine that their needs are not being met—as happened at the early stages of our CI—the group can then make necessary changes.

The evaluation must occur within each session and over time. Each meeting must end with a discussion of what was learned through the process and how it has helped participants clarify issues or problems. If one participant is unable to do so, then the whole group can work to help that participant make connections. It will seriously undermine the subsequent CI if participants are confused or unsatisfied when they leave a session.

Similarly, at the end of the entire CI, time must be set aside for a discussion of the process's effectiveness in terms of participants' learning, practice, and leadership. A CI that fosters learning but does not motivate participants to apply that learning to their practice or their leadership development has not reached its full potential. For this reason the cycles of action-reflection-action are crucial, so that participants can make clear connections between the group process and their own leadership. As mentioned in Chapter 4, knowing if and when the research question has been answered is also an opportunity to evaluate the CI. How the question has been answered and to the extent that participants agree that they are able to understand and apply the knowledge gained through the process will determine how "good" the CI has been.

Last, a facilitator needs to model this evaluation process by openly seeking feedback from the participants about his or her facilitation. By taking "action" into their practice, facilitators model reflection and learning in a way that fosters the improvement of the facilitation and the group process. This also demonstrates that "evaluation" is a learning tool, not, as many see it, a punitive process that focuses on what is *not* being accomplished. By honestly seeking the input of the group—individually and collectively—facilitators not only improve their practice, but also pave the way for the group and participants to evaluate themselves.

BECOMING A CO-INQUIRER

Throughout this chapter the focus has been on what the facilitator must do to engage participants in a CI. There has also been mention, indirectly, of when and how the facilitator can "let go" of some aspects of facilitation in order to empower participants and to begin moving into the role of co-inquirer. What we have not discussed directly is what *co-inquiry* means for facilitators and for the larger issue of continued facilitation.

Facilitator inquiry. At some point in the CI, the facilitator moves from the role of facilitator to one of *co-inquirer*, depending on the needs of participants and the inquiry. This transition to co-inquirer is not necessarily smooth or easy. The facilitator/co-inquirer does not relinquish the role completely or cease to focus on learning and participation. The role of the facilitator continues to be important, particularly in times of transition. But as participants begin to take on some of the role of facilitation, the facilitator is "freed up" to become involved in the inquiry itself, to focus on his or her own leadership question and learning.

The issues of empowerment and relationship are particularly relevant here. Throughout, the facilitator has worked to create a physical and mental space where participants come to make the CI their own, where they "own" the question, the process, and the outcomes. In doing this, the facilitator has built relationships with participants and has helped them to look to one another for guidance (the independent-interdependent dynamic discussed earlier). Just as the CI requires participants to trust one another and to work together to tackle an essential leadership question, so must the facilitator trust the participants to become co-inquirers, to inquire *with* them. This is the ultimate test of whether participants have truly been empowered. To some degree, if the facilitator is successful in this, they have facilitated themselves out of a job!

Facilitator learning. To facilitate the learning of *others* it is necessary to talk about *facilitator* learning. Discussed previously was the role of the facilitator in modeling necessary skills. At the heart of this modeling is the importance of being a learner—learning not just in relation to the content of the inquiry (in this case, urban leadership), but also in terms of becoming a new kind of facilitator. In the process of learning, each facilitator will meet her or his own roadblocks and challenges. For example, facilitators who dwell on logistical issues could be throwing up a roadblock to their participation or learning. Disciplining oneself to focus on the inquiry and participant learning requires a heightened level of awareness. It also requires engaging in cycles of action and reflection into one's own practice as facilitator (including doing research into one's own "question").

A final note on facilitation. Facilitation as we practice and envision it, poses a unique challenge for facilitators. Traditionally, the facilitator guides participants to a specific point. To do that, the facilitator must do many of the things that we have discussed here (such as question posing and meeting needs of participants). There are two essential differences. The first is that in CI the facilitator does not know what the "specific point" is. There is no way of knowing that "when participants do that, I do this." As we have mentioned many times, there is no clear blueprint for CI or CI facilitation. The power of CI lies in the fact that it goes where it goes!

This leads to the second difference that is the inherent tension in the role of facilitator. Unlike "traditional" approaches to facilitation whereby the role is clearly defined ("I need to get you to point X and I know how best to get you there"), in CI the role is amorphous and changing, and facilitators must be able to juggle several balls. At times the facilitator is the "knower," at other times the "baffled," at others the "questioner," at others the "questioned," at others the leader, at others the follower. And central to these multiple facets is the joint journey, as in "how do we find out where we want to go and what is the best way or ways of getting there together?" The tension created by playing multiple roles, by not always being sure of the destination—but confident in the journey—and by the evolving nature of the roles is something that needs to be acknowledged and managed by individual facilitators.

SUMMARY AND IMPLICATIONS

In this chapter we have taken a closer look at the role of the facilitator/co-inquirer. Unlike Chapter 4, where we discussed some of the more "nuts and bolts" aspects of facilitating a CI, here we have discussed the affective skills or dispositions necessary for facilitation. It is these dispositions, along with understanding potential roadblocks, that allow the facilitator to focus on the more important elements of participant engagement and development. Through careful attention to structure and learning, the facilitator is able to empower participants and, ultimately, become a co-inquirer.

The role of facilitator should not be ignored or underappreciated in CI. As an integral member of the group, the facilitator brings to the table skills and dispositions that will seriously affect the development of the group and the CI. It is important to note that skills often valued in other forms of facilitation (e.g., clear direction, information providing), are undesirable in CI. This "new" kind of facilitation requires a degree of comfort with ambiguity and the capacity to act in ways that may be counterinstinctual (i.e., letting participants "struggle" with their question, follow participants in order to help them make sense of their experience), especially for experienced facilitators. This in turn requires that facilitators be *hyper*aware of themselves, the purposes of CI, and the learning needs of participants. Without this awareness a CI can quickly devolve into a "really interesting meeting" and not evolve into a dynamic leadership development catalyst.

Perhaps one of the most important things that a facilitator can do in CI is work with participants to turn their learning into action—"action" not just in doing something differently at work based on group discussion and reflection, but also in actively developing their leadership. Without the larger "leadership" framework, participants will become better practitioners and increase their ability to see problems in new ways, but they may not integrate this into a better understanding of their own leadership. Participants in this CI convened around practical questions (i.e., relationship with the district, instruction), but these questions revolved around the "bigger" issue of what it takes to lead an urban school. It is this bigger question that goes to the heart of school leadership in any context. And it is this bigger question that will ultimately improve schools.

CHAPTER 6

Conclusions

DRAWING TO A CLOSE

The facilitator, noting the lateness of the hour and evening plans that various participants had stated they had when starting the CI, suggests that it is time to stop. "We have been talking for almost two hours," she says, "and Anye has a parent meeting to attend tonight, and Josue had wanted to get home early today." Still, the participants linger. A few continue the conversation started in the CI, reiterating points they had made and pressing the problem holder to anticipate how he was going to put his new strategies into action. A few others trade information about people they know in common and their plans on how to benefit from an upcoming mandated leadership meeting.

The collaborative inquiry process serves as a powerful vehicle for individual principal learning through collective inquiry and problem solving. In turn, what the principals learn and how they learn it provides many benefits for them and for their schools. Collaborative inquiry, particularly as modeled and outlined in this book, can serve well as a critical leadership development strategy within a broader district improvement and reform effort, particularly when linked with an educational vision and direction. The challenges to using this process, however, are inherent in its principles of trust, learning through questioning rather than directives, and democratic and sustained participation. This chapter elaborates the benefits, uses, and challenges to be considered in future use of this model.

BENEFITS OF CI FOR PARTICIPANTS

As the meeting ending illustrates, at its heart, CI is about fostering camaraderie and learning for those in a role that often involves limited learning opportunities and highly idiosyncratic working conditions and organizational challenges. Through CI, as we found with our participants, principals gain new insights, knowledge, and skills, as well as a capacity to tailor possible solutions to their unique contexts and schools' needs. Principals' learning through CI is both complex and iterative and evolves throughout the process. It is a supportive, inquiry-based process, rather than a competitive and faultfinding one. Consequently, the principals invest more in one another's successes and learning generally, benefiting from the process, in that this enriches them professionally and sustains them personally.

The primary benefits for participants lie in the enrichment of their work, as a result of what they learn. Principals have the potential to gain five types of knowledge, skills, and frames through CI: (1) organizational knowledge about rules, regulations, their interpretation, and normative expectations; (2) new professional practice ideas (such as new models of staff development); (3) new perspectives for problem framing; (4) educational improvement and change; and (5) leadership. In our CI experience, principals from large districts also learned important organizational survival strategies in a complex environment of central district demands and state and local accountability pressures: how and when to be organizational compliant, how to be entrepreneurial and garner much needed resources, how to negotiate conflicting central office demands and initiatives while maintaining an instructional improvement focus, and how to maintain a sense of self and one's own leadership integrity.

Often, principals' skill development was related to the context of their district and policy. Frequently, discussions centered on understanding and managing the complexity of change, given pressures to adopt systemic reform strategies and standards-based curriculum. Most challenging for the participants was working through the tension between required reform efforts and what works for their schools. The CI forum gave them space to explore these tensions and develop strategies. As a result, participants often discussed skills needed to improve instruction, supervise teachers, and continue the process of change, all of which benefited their schools.

As the group gains experience in solving problems, their focus shifts to the larger, more abstract levels of the problems and leadership concerns and become more sophisticated in their inquiry and analysis. The first type of learning begins with what was described by Reason (in Bray et al., 2000) as "making sense," in which individual learning occurs through asking the question "How can I understand what I have been through?" (p. 88). It evolves over time into what Mezirow (1991) describes as "making meaning," in which participants attempt to "construe or interpret experience" (p. 88) in order to give it coherence and be able to integrate it into their learning. Both these learning processes require identification of patterns in their leadership, personal theory building, and knowledge construction. The problems that participants present are often vehicles for larger questions and learning about their roles and their leadership, in addition to the more concrete demands of the job. Through the in-depth discussions of leadership dilemmas, participants point out to one another recurring behaviors or underlying assumptions that help them to better understand their experiences and lead to new perspectives. Further, the work of a group typically moves from an exchange of concrete information to more abstract discussions of roles, identities, and future goals.

Problem-solving skills improve as well. Over time, the group will shift from initiating problem solving when problems of practice are posed, to spending more significant time identifying and understanding a problem first, even reframing it into a different type of problem for solution generation. The CI process itself also enables them to learn to help others consider solutions rather than their simply solving the problem for them.

Thus, CI changes how participants work together. Specifically, our participants came to value their CI experience in terms of their practice and socialization, personal development, and creation of a support system. The personal and professional costs of their role were discussed many times during the CI as they explored ways of achieving a healthy balance between work and family. The "personal" was also important for career planning and management. Within the group, participants articulated and discussed long-term goals. Moreover, CI provided a means by which principals could reflect upon themselves within their role and on the impact of their role on their lives. Our work has shown that ignoring the personal experience and knowledge that participants bring to their professional lives undermines their potential and their learning. Similarly, to disregard long-term professional goals and implications for personal lives belittles participants' needs. When participants make connections between their professional and personal lives through peer-based collaborative discussions, their commitment to their practice, their role, and their peers is strengthened, thus breaking the isolation that has plagued school leaders for so long.

IMPLICATIONS OF CI AS LEADERSHIP DEVELOPMENT

By incorporating structured reflection, critical thinking, and creative problem solving into the context of current leadership situations, CI as professional development builds on elements that are essential to adult learning: drawing on one's lived experiences, individual and group reflection, and developing working theories with which to frame and enlighten experiences.

CI is a flexible process that enables principals to resolve the tension created by the demands of school and district leadership and their own developing capacities to improve their schools' performance and effectiveness. CI merges issues rising from the district context, leadership theory, and adult learning, thereby facilitating leadership development and socialization of principals into their roles and contexts.

The strength of CI as a professional development tool lies in its focus on participant learning, through larger questions about the nature of effective practice and through individual problem exploration and problem-solving experiences. As such, the process provides many "entry points" for participants' learning, through their own problems, through the problems of others, and through reflection on the process at each session and over time.

The focus on learning, and on the learner, has several implications for the "practice" of professional development. The first is the role of the facilitator, not as expert but as co-learner. And while professional developers have knowledge about a particular strategy or area, they are often inexperienced within a specific context. The importance of using a mutually compelling question as a way of framing the experience shifts the focus from passive delivery of information to active group learning. Positioning oneself as learner allows both facilitators and participants to use information and experience sharing as a vehicle for creating new knowledge and a community of learners.

A second implication is that of the relationship between action and reflection as inherent in the learning process. By carving time out to do deep reflection and emphasizing problem framing, participants are given the opportunity to understand their practice and perspectives and see possible consequences for their leadership and school improvement work. The subsequent problem solving—or action—gave our participants a set of options for improving their work, as well as a sense of confidence when they returned to their school. Follow-up discussions allowed participants to reflect once more on the outcomes of their actions and to see the applicability of those strategies to other new situations. Within this framework, learning relies on these cycles of action and reflection.

Third, principal professional development cannot truly be understood or implemented without careful consideration of the context in which it occurs. The dynamic nature of the environment that principals constantly face—particularly those in low-performing and urban schools—such as the expansion of their role, conflicting demands, implementing mandated reform, finding support, and problems of extreme community poverty, are critical to their ability to grow and develop both personally and professionally. The impact that the internal and external environments have on the relationship between professional development opportunities and strategies and the reality of principals and their school improvement work cannot be underestimated.

A final implication is that of the relationship between content and process and the necessary strength to be "organic" when approaching professional development. An appreciation of the dynamic between content and process, and the time—and patience—necessary to truly foster learning is at the heart of this perspective on professional development.

CHALLENGES

This approach to professional development, however, is challenging as a *process,* from creating a CI group to the inquiry process itself, and as a *conceptual* endeavor. First is the importance of having a strategy to shift the group from a collection of individuals to one with strong group identity, trust, and engagement. Initial trust and respect for at least one other participant and the opportunity to work closely together were two of the main motivations for joining the group.

Another process challenge was in developing a process that would value and build on participants' experiences and knowledge, yet would also challenge their current thinking and practices. All the participants, including facilitators, had to be able to look critically at both the inquiry process and the group process, since the two are interdependent. Similarly, all the participants had to be able to make process changes when necessary during the inquiry.

CI is a change in how professional development for participants as well as facilitators is conceived. Several participants did not initially view the CI approach as a form of professional development because it was so different from anything they had experienced before. Yet they all recognized the role of the inquiry experience in their learning and their practice. The focus of the inquiry on their leadership, and subsequent discussions of their learning, was a new experience for several participants as well. This was reflected in their initial expectations, and for some participants their initial disappointment, to share strategies. The CI also required that participants look at their own learning differently and see it as connected to their leadership. This posed another conceptual challenge for participants and facilitators alike. Consequently, not everyone learns equally well through this process.

Another significant challenge is the amount of time needed for an in-depth exploration into participants' practice and their learning. Given the current climate, which focuses on immediate results, it is uncertain how many other principals or organizations would commit themselves to that length of time for a professional development experience.

INCORPORATING CI INTO SCHOOL AND DISTRICT DEVELOPMENT

While CI can be a powerful vehicle for enhancing the leadership capacity of individual principals, it can become a significant engine for enhancing their collective capacity for districtwide leadership development and as a platform for the district to become a learning organization. First, it provides a model of professional learning that principals can replicate. Participating in a CI of this nature enables principals to experience directly a powerful professional development approach that they can use as a complement to their building-level professional development for teachers and administrators. Second, it provides a means by which principals can explore district priorities; their roles; and implementation expectations, opportunities, and challenges. Such exploration enables principals to look beyond mere compliance with district expectations to engaging with theories of action and change. Third, it fosters a capacity for principals to work collectively, thereby strengthening leadership relations within the district and reinforcing shared expectations for mutual problem solving and support.

Districts that are committed to school improvement must give priority to developing school leaders of all kinds. By focusing on the leadership necessary for understanding and responding to changing schools and districts, professional development can contribute significantly to the quality and effectiveness of reform and improvement efforts. There are many ways, therefore, that districts can incorporate CI into their leadership development efforts:

- Providing the opportunity and resources (including facilitation) for principals to meet voluntarily for collaborative inquiry
- Setting aside time regularly in administrative meetings for collaborative inquiry discussions on problems of practices
- Adapting the CI approach to questions about new strategies for district and school reform (e.g., how to close the achievement gap or how to improve differentiated instruction) that would supplement school and district improvement priorities

Its use as a district improvement strategy, however, requires the integration of its underlying principles—learning orientation, continuous improvement, and collaboration—into the district's overall approach to reform and improvement. Moreover, this work needs sufficient support and resources, through facilitation, time for the inquiry, and space. Finally, it requires confidence in the process—a belief that it will yield important learning and knowledge as well as skill development—without the prescription that reform work typically entails.

Through our experience with CI, we learned not just about our roles as facilitators, but also about the leadership development needs of principals and the importance of co-creating professional learning experiences with principals. The demand for principal professional development that strengthens individual skills but also shapes and improves organizations is everywhere in education. In a time of mounting pressures caused by changing demographics, by the need for a new kind of global "learner," and by increased accountability, they require that districts and professional development providers also evolve into new ways of thinking about learning and developing leadership. We believe that CI is one vehicle for doing so. We also believe that many principals, educators, and parents feel a sense of urgency in improving our schools to meet the challenges, not just of individual students, but of entire communities. Developing school leaders is key to meeting the needs of our changing educational world.

APPENDIX A

Vignettes

This appendix offers a snapshot of the kinds of issues and challenges that participants brought to the group. These problems ranged from building-level concerns, district initiatives, and external pressures. By using the CI, participants were better able to understand the dynamics of their problems and work together to develop new solutions.

ROCKY RELATIONSHIPS

The superintendent. Kevin's relationship with the superintendent is quickly deteriorating. A self-styled "old-school" principal, Kevin prides himself on his hands-on approach to discipline and his skill at controlling students. Leading instruction is something that he leaves to the teachers. He has been brought into the middle school to phase out the existing school and coordinate with the incoming school leadership. His nickname in the district is "the Closer." During his time at the school, there have been several complaints about his relationship with students and parents. The suspension rate at the school has finally come to the attention of the superintendent. His meetings with the superintendent have resulted in open confrontations. Kevin thinks that the superintendent is "out to get him" and he is "digging in" to meet this challenge to his leadership.

The union representative. From the moment Nicole became principal of the school, she has met with resistance from the teachers' union representative (union rep). When she took her first principal-ship 6 months earlier she knew that the union rep had personal ties to the superintendent. She includes the union rep in leadership meetings and tries to meet with her regularly to keep her informed of Nicole's school improvement plans. In faculty meetings Nicole makes sure that she recognizes the contributions of the union rep. Despite these efforts, Nicole is dismayed that the rep has filed several grievances against her with the district. In addition, other members of her staff inform her that the union rep continues to instigate defiance among the teachers, stalling her improvement efforts.

MAINTAINING FOCUS

District turmoil. Sheila is the senior principal in her district. It is her 3rd year. The superintendent who hired her left the district the previous year amid much controversy. Several principals at the elementary and middle school levels have either retired or left the district, leaving vacancies across the district. The new superintendent has taken the existing leadership vacuum as an opportunity to move the remaining principals around to other schools and to give priority to improving the high schools. To that end, she brought in a new leadership team who has specialized in high school reform. District gossip says that her motive for improving the high school is to catapult herself into a state-level position. As new elementary principals are hired in the district, they turn to Sheila for curriculum assistance, since the new assistant superintendent has no K–6 experience. In her first 2 years, Sheila managed to improve her own school's culture and performance. She is not sure why the superintendent chose to leave her in her school. But as more of her time is consumed by assisting other principals, she worries about the possible negative consequences for her school.

Advocating building needs. Josue successfully led his school off the statewide school improvement list in less than 3 years. When the school was placed on the list almost 3 years earlier, the then principal had been removed and the district took a "special interest" in the school. Despite the fact that Josue was brought on with the mandate to "shake things up," he feels that his decisions are scrutinized at every level. District personnel come to the school on a biweekly basis and leave after a cursory visit. A month later he receives a "report" that recommends strategies for improvement. The fourth-grade teachers in particular resent these visits from virtual strangers who know nothing about their classes or the work they are doing. Josue also views these visits and reports with skepticism, although they occasionally contain interesting and useful ideas. More often than not, however, he grits his teeth when "suggestions" are something that his school implemented months earlier. Up until now he has been able to respond to district reform directives based on the needs of his staff and students, often piecing together strategies from the report with current school initiatives. This morning, however, he received a strange message saying that the superintendent wanted to meet with him first thing in the morning to discuss recent reports. He was told to bring his school improvement plan. The tone of the message left him worried.

CONTINUOUS IMPROVEMENT

Geoffrey, Anye, Nicole, and Josue have successfully led their schools off the statewide improvement list. They have brushed off accolades and focused attention on teacher and student efforts. Recently, however, they have noticed a level of complacency in their buildings that raised some warning flags. As they do their walk-throughs they see an increasing number of worksheet-based lessons and students off task. Their staff developers have also reported that attendance at grade-level team meetings has started to decline and that grade-level planning has become sporadic. In addition, when reviewing test data for the past few years, they noticed that while there is improvement in some areas, other areas seem to have plateaued (especially for some of the subgroups). Initially they thought that after the final push in preparation for the statewide test, the teachers needed a breather. But when the level of complacency is coupled with the analysis of test data, they worry that maybe teachers feel that the current level of success is enough. It was easy to motivate teachers when the threat of state turnover hung over them. Now, without the imminent threat, the principals find themselves in new territory and uncertain of how to continue the cycle of improvement.

MANAGING THE MEDIA

Anye's school has been at the heart of a media maelstrom. Recently, the print press decided to run a series of exposés on school safety. When a journalist requested a meeting with her, she was willing. Several colleagues have told her to make the media her "friend," since they can sway public opinion for or against her school. She knew the meeting was going to be about school safety. In preparation, she took out the school safety plan that she had submitted to the district at the beginning of the year. Overall, Anye is confident in the "safeness" of her school: Visitors are screened by the school safety officer, teachers and staff have school badges, and hallways are regularly patrolled by administrators and safety officers. She has had no violent incidents occur in the building in the past year and her suspension rate is the lowest in the district. This meeting is her opportunity to present district schools, and her school in particular, in a good light. The reporter arrives and they exchange pleasantries. She is caught completely off guard, therefore, when the reporter shows her a video of his entering the building through a side door that had been left ajar. The video shows how he walked around the building to her office, passing the safety officer and other staff without being stopped. The reporter turns the video off and asks Anye to respond.

CAREER MANAGEMENT

Geoffrey is a successful principal. He left his last school, a middle school, after successfully implementing some school improvement strategies. His work at the district level and his doctoral studies made him feel confident in his ability to turn the school around. The school was beginning to show improvement on multiple measures (including state tests) when he was recruited to lead an elementary school. He is starting his 3rd year at his current school, all the time implementing many of the same improvement strategies: building beautification, individual professional development meetings with teachers, grade-level team planning, community outreach, and grant writing. The school has received local and even national attention from multiple media sources for its quick turnaround. Educators from around the country visit the school to learn about its success, and recently, international educators have visited as well. Geoffrey has been recognized by organizations ranging from the parent association to the district as Principal of the Year. In addition, he has been selected to serve as an advisor on national principal panels. At this juncture, Geoffrey is looking for ways to leverage his success into a superintendent position.

APPRECIATIVE INQUIRY

Geoffrey and the other participants meet one evening to talk about the success they have experienced in their schools. The idea came from a previous meeting when it was raised that they never talk about what works for them. While the focus on their leadership dilemmas is useful and they have learned a great deal from one another, the question was raised about whether they could also learn from what they already did well. Despite agreeing that success is often "fleeting" and not to be trusted, they decide to spend time studying their successes. Of the six principals in the group, four have managed to lead their schools in continuous improvement. Three have been named Principal of the Year. They begin by sharing their recent successes. As they compare and analyze their experiences, they realize that they have applied similar strategies (e.g., aligning resources, creating support structures, providing opportunities for teacher leadership) in different contexts and to varying degrees.

Then they compare their success strategies to recent problems. From their discussion they realize that often the difference between "success" and "not success" is dependent on how well they have consistently applied these strategies and the degree to which they have been integrated into all aspects of school efforts. The question then becomes, How do I focus my energy to plan for success?

How to Conduct CI as Professional Development

This appendix offers some suggested guidelines for those interested in using CI as part of a district improvement plan. It includes issues of timing, group size, roles, a few helpful protocols, a year-long schedule, and seminar agendas. These guidelines are shared in order to help facilitators—and other interested stakeholders—to maintain an inquiry approach within a professional development context.

TIMING AND GROUP SIZE

To allow the necessary time for the CI to be effective, we recommend meeting once a month for the entire academic year. Each meeting should be a minimum of 2 hours in length, which should allow for one full cycle of problem discussion (as discussed in Chapter 2) and reflection. The group should range from between six and eight participants; more than that and levels of engagement and comfort will vary markedly.

In Chapter 5, we discussed at length the role of the facilitator and the skills/dispositions needed for successful facilitation. It is essential that facilitators be present at all the meetings and make themselves available to speak with participants between seminars. While we also advocated for co-facilitation, it is clear that the local context will determine the number of facilitators as well as the size of the CI group. In the event that the group is larger than eight participants, we would strongly recommend co-facilitators.

ROLES

There are no formal roles in CI. However, groups may feel the need to identify certain responsibilities that group members can take. One of those roles can be that of timekeeping. This is particularly important in the early iterations of the CI until the group becomes comfortable with the process. Once participants have internalized the process, the role of timekeeper is diminished. Another role that can help group learning is that of summarizing the meeting. This role allows participants to focus their learning and also build individual skills. Groups should determine other roles that they feel are necessary to help their learning.

INTRODUCING CI

For those attempting CI for the first time, explaining what "it is" may be challenging. The first recommendation would be to read as many cases of CI as possible (see Bray et al., 2000; Reason, 1994). From these cases, identify key areas (e.g., the relationship between CI and practice) that are most relevant to the leadership context. This will also give you a deeper understanding of CI. These key areas and applications can then be shared with interested participants as a foundation for future work. In addition to focusing on practice, it is also necessary to focus on the importance on group and individual learning as a means of improving practice. As a result it is important to elicit individual goals as soon as possible in order to make sure that the CI works for participants.

PROTOCOLS

During the course of the CI, several protocols were adopted, and adapted, to facilitate learning. In particular, protocols from Partners for Learning and Leadership (www.partnersforlearning.com) were employed to guide the use of time and to provide a framework for participants as they acquired the necessary CI skills.

Time. Here is the timing protocol that was adapted for this CI (for more detailed format, see the Partners for Learning website, given above). These times are aligned with the components discussed in Chapter 2.

Problem sharing and selection	10–12 minutes
Problem exploration	20–25 minutes
Problem reframing	10–15 minutes
Problem solving applications	10–15 minutes
Problem solving implications	10–15 minutes

Questions. Problem exploration through question posing is essential to fostering CI and learning. When the group is working through a problem, questions become the means for understanding relevant information and for reframing the problem. According to Partners for Learning, questions can be divided into four perspectives: objective, reflective, interpretive, and decisional (Figure B.1). These questions allow participants to avoid framing solutions as questions and to provide a deeper analysis of the problem being presented.

Assumptions. Uncovering assumptions is essential to the process of understanding the problem. Uncovering assumptions, however, takes time and practice. Assumptions are what we believe to be true about an issue or problem. One way to uncover assumptions is to have participants put themselves in the "shoes" of the problem holder and think about what they would believe is going on. Through the sharing of assumptions of the group, the problem holder can see what assumptions group members are holding. Once assumptions are shared and discussed, participants begin to see other ways of understanding the problem.

Reframing. Reframing is based on more detailed understanding of the problem and the problem context, as well as from uncovered assumptions. As stated earlier, these help participants to "see" the problem in new ways. Another useful tool is applying organizational lenses to the problems (see Bolman & Deal, 1997). These lenses help increase participants' understanding by using multiple

Figure B.1. Types of problem-exploration questions.

Objective	Reflective	Interpretive	Decisional
Requires the problem holder to add more detail for problem analysis:	*Helps the problem holder identify motivations and goals:*	*Allows the problem holder to make sense of what has oc-curred and see implications:*	*Focuses the problem holder on action and possible solutions:*
Can you describe more ...?	What were you thinking when ...?	What have you learned so far?	What's stopping you from ...?
What else was happening when ...?	Would it make any difference if ...?	How would you know if ...?	What can you do differently?
Who are the stakeholders?	What did you hope to achieve?	What are the implications of ...?	What will you do next?

Source: Adapted from the Partners for Learning and Leadership website (www.partnersforlearning.com).

perspectives to further analyze the problem. Given this new under-standing of the problem, participants often come to see the "real" problem as something other than what was originally perceived.

Learning norms. Learning norms are best discussed and decided upon by participants. It is difficult to impose norms for learning before the group has defined learning. The following questions may help participants to think about their learning as a precursor to de-veloping norms.

- How does working in a group contribute to your learning?
- What makes a group not be productive for your learning?
- What learning norms would you propose for the group's work?

After sharing and discussing the responses to these questions, learning norms can be developed. Here is a sample of learning norms:

- Avoid dominating the session
- Maintain open dialogue and communication
- Practice active listening
- Respect all voices
- Ask for a summary when needed

We recommend that the learning norms be established in the second or third session, after the group members have become fa-miliar with CI and each other.

YEAR-LONG PROFESSIONAL DEVELOPMENT PLAN

Below is an outline of a year-long sequence of sessions.

First seminar. The purpose of this first seminar is to introduce CI to interested participants. This requires that facilitators (1) under-stand the potential of CI as a tool for professional development and

(2) provide a clear explanation of what CI is. This first meeting is part of the "invitation" discussed in Chapter 4.

AGENDA

- Orient the group conceptually and instrumentally.
- Discuss the district's reform context, its challenges, and participants' questions about leading learning in this context.
- Elicit personal/professional goals for learning/leadership development.
- Explore the potential for CI and focusing questions.
- Propose next steps.
- Final reflection.

Second seminar. This second seminar is designed to allow participants to identify a guiding question (or questions) and to experience a full CI cycle. Since it is the first time that participants will be engaging in a CI, expect it to take longer, and allow for participants to ask process questions. Also, in this session be sure to be more active in guiding the final reflection so that participants make connections between the CI, their work, and their leadership question. This seminar represents the beginning of the "initiation" phase (see Chapter 4).

AGENDA

- Revisit preceding meeting by checking understanding of CI, responding to questions, and reexamining personal/professional goals.
- Review leadership questions, and identify some possible guiding questions.
- Conduct first CI.
- Participant reflection on learning, process (including own role), and connections to their leadership of district reform.
- Determine next steps.

Third seminar. This seminar should (1) finalize the inquiry question, (2) determine learning norms, and (3) encompass a second CI. Similar to the second seminar, the CI may take more time than originally thought. The facilitator must help participants become aware of the kinds of questions being asked. In addition, the facilitator must again ensure that the final reflection focuses on understanding the inquiry question. The seminar is often the conclusion of the "initiation" phase (see Chapter 4).

AGENDA

- Revisit preceding meeting, and determine guiding question(s).
- Establish learning norms (explain this).
- Problem holder from previous session updates group.
- Conduct second CI.
- Participant reflection on learning and connection to their leadership of district reform.
- Determine next steps.

Fourth through ninth seminars. These seminars follow much the same agenda, in that participants continue to explore their leadership dilemmas through CI and gather "data" on answering the inquiry question. As participants become more comfortable with the CI process the role of the facilitator becomes less pronounced. The facilitator, however, must continue to be aware of helping participants make connection between the CI and the inquiry question. These sessions represent the "duration" phase of the CI (see Chapter 4).

AGENDA

- Revisit preceding meeting.
- Review learning norms as needed.
- Problem holder from previous session updates group.
- Conduct CI.

- Participant reflection on learning and connection to their leadership of district reform.
- Determine next steps.

Final seminar. This final seminar is the "conclusion" phase of the CI (see Chapter 4). During this session participants finalize the answer to the inquiry question, raise any unresolved questions, reflect on their personal/professional goals, and discuss ways in which to share the results of the CI with others (in their schools, with colleagues, or within the district). In addition, the group may want to discuss other ways, or other contexts, in which CI can be useful in developing leadership or furthering district reform.

AGENDA

- Do a CI on the CI—how has the CI answered the guiding question(s)? What have participants learned and applied to their work?
- Reflect on CI's role in advancing the district's reforms, addressing challenges, and developing its leadership.
- Evaluate personal/professional benefits for learning/leadership development.
- Explore the potential for CI in other contexts and for participants' coming year's work.
- Celebrate.
- Propose future steps.

How to Conduct CI as Research

While we have described CI as a form of professional development for school leaders, it is also used as a research method. It is grounded in action learning and qualitative research methodologies. Its aim is to create insight into a question or interest in order to

> (1) [understand] your world, make sense of your life and develop new and creative ways of looking at things; and (2) learn how to act to change things you may want to change and find out how to do things better. (Heron & Reason, 2001, p. 179)

According to Heron (1996), there are four ways of knowing:

- *Experiential knowing*, that is, through direct face-to-face encounter with a person place or thing.
- *Presentational knowing*, which emerges from experiential knowing and is a form of expressing meaning and significance through imagery (such as in poetry, stories, or drawing).
- *Propositional knowing*, which comes from knowing through ideas and theories as a means of knowing about something.
- *Practical knowing*, which is knowing that is expressed through how we do something, such as a skill or competence.

Heron and Reason (2001) argue that our knowing becomes more valid if these four ways are congruent with one another. Gaining such congruence, particularly in leading to practical knowledge and its manifestation, is the aim of CI research. Thus, the inquiry cycles purposefully evolve through these ways of knowing, enabling participants to gain both insight and inquiry skill.

GROUPS AND PARTICIPANTS

Collaborative inquiry begins with a group of people who have a shared inquiry interest, including some who are internal to the proposed topic as a field of study or practice. A typical CI group has six to eight participants, large enough to have diverse views but small enough for all to actively engage in the discussions. Groups can be structured so that all co-researchers have similar roles or as mixed roles. Groups can be created as opened or closed— depending on whether other inquirers can be allowed in at later points and how much the group members interact with their wider world of practice.

The participants in CI research have the dual role of researcher and research population. CI does not do research on people, but rather with and for the people involved (Heron, 1981; Reason, 1988). In essence, it "is an aware and self-critical movement between experience and reflection which goes through several cycles as ideas, practice, and [in which] experiences are systematically honed and refined" (Reason, 1988, p. 6). Through this process of participant as researcher and subject, knowledge is generated from the lives and experiences of participants.

RESEARCH QUESTION

CI as research begins with a question or idea that guides the inquiry. Such a question needs to be meaningful enough to engage the participants' time and energy and should be relevant to their field of work and experiences.

DATA COLLECTION AND ANALYSIS

In grounded theory, data collection and analysis are deeply inter-twined. Information is "gathered" and "analyzed" through a series of questionings, conversations, and meaning makings. Each inquiry is viewed as a cycle of question investigation. Participants continue through this cycle until "the initial questions are fully answered in practice" (Reason, 1994, p. 44).

According to Heron and Reason (2001), collaborative inquiry (or cooperative inquiry, as they term it) cycles through four phases of reflection and action:

- *Phase 1.* A group comes together around an essential ques-tion or agreed-upon area to be explored. In this phase, par-ticipants agree to engage in the inquiry, establish their focus, and generate an initial set of questions or propositions that they wish to investigate. As part of this inquiry, they may devise a related set of procedures for gathering and record-ing data on the focus of their inquiry.
- *Phase 2.* In this phase, the co-researchers or participants may gather the information they might need to facilitate their in-quiry, such as through observation, interviews, or other data collection means.
- *Phase 3.* The co-researchers are full immersed in this phase, in which they may pursue practical applications of new in-sights or uncover new problems, and may be led by their insights into new areas, actions, and creative insights. The group provides a means of support and reflection through-out this phase.
- *Phase 4.* In this phase, the co-researchers share—in both pre-sentational and propositional forms—their practical and ex-periential findings. Through the inquiry process, they reflect upon their initial ideas, reframing them or posing new ones. This process may lead to new areas of inquiry. This phase may include several cycles of reflection and action, balancing

divergence and convergence on specific parts or the whole of the original ideas.

INFORMED CONSENT

Unlike in conventional research, the form and nature of the questions throughout the CI are emergent and thus cannot be fully revealed initially. Consequently, gaining participants' informed consent to a CI study focuses on the inquiry process and the likelihood that it will lead in multiple possible directions. In our practice, when CI is used for research purposes, participants must understand the guiding research question, the nature of the CI process, and the uses intended for the study findings. In addition, participants should be given the opportunity to reflect upon preliminary conclusions throughout the inquiry process (as this aids the inquiry itself) and collaborate in writing and reviewing drafts at the study's conclusion. Participants' roles in each phase of the study should be clarified as part of the informed consent, and they should have the opportunity to withdraw at any time.

DATA ANALYSIS

The traditions of grounded theory (Miles & Huberman, 1994; Strauss & Corbin, 1990), case study research (Yin, 2002), and focus group data analysis techniques (Krueger, 1994) provide useful strategies for facilitating data analysis throughout the CI process. These data analysis approaches similarly use an iterative analysis process, starting with constructing a clear analytic story and focusing on key concepts, themes, and patterns in the discussions. Through a review and discussion of these over time, the participants can begin to construct a framework and examine relationships, drawing on available theory as is relevant.

The repeating cycles of reflection and action, as well as the collaboration among co-researchers, enhance the validity of the findings.

Notes

Chapter 1

1. Principals in large districts are increasingly more likely to be female and non-White than are principals in smaller districts (Fiore & Curtin, 1997; Shen, Rodriguez-Campos, & Rincones-Gomez, 2000).

Chapter 2

1. We adopted this level of assumption questioning from Victoria Marsick's action learning protocol (2002).

2. We use Heifetz and Linsky's (2001) definition of adaptive change and adaptive leadership. According to them, leadership is the activity of mobilizing adaptive work or meeting adaptive challenges, using authority, power, and influence. It is not about maintaining equilibrium but on meeting new challenges and demands effectively through supporting what should be sustained, removing what is expendable, and developing what is needed. Adaptive leadership is well explained in Heifetz and Linsky (2001).

3. Appreciative inquiry is defined as a collaborative inquiry in search of the best in people, their organizations, and the relevant world around them to understand what makes it most effective and capable. It uses questions and a four-stage process to understand, anticipate, and strengthen the organization's positive potential. Appreciative inquiry is based on the work in Cooperrider and Whitney (2005).

Chapter 3

1. It is important to note that collaborative inquiry, as we have used it, builds on the work of John Heron and Peter Reason beginning in the 1980s. Heron and Reason developed *cooperative* inquiry as a way of engaging in research *with* people, not *on* or *for* them. They sought to redefine research as a democratic process that

included the researcher and the subject in an equal relationship based on mutual need. This philosophical and conceptual approach to conducting research has interesting implications for providing professional development, as will be discussed below. For purposes of clarity, the term *collaborative inquiry* is used when applying the research method as a model for professional development.

References

Bezzina, M. (1994). *Empowering the principal through professional development.* Paper presented at the Australian Teacher Education Association Conference.

Bolman, L., & Deal, T. (1997). *Reframing organizations: Artistry, choice, and leadership.* San Francisco: Jossey-Bass.

Bray, J., Lee, J., Smith, L., & Yorks, L. (2000). *Collaborative inquiry in practice.* Thousand Oaks, CA: Sage.

Brookfield, S. (1987). *Developing critical thinkers.* San Francisco: Jossey-Bass.

Brown, J. S., & Duguid, P. (1991). Organizational learning and communities of practice: Towards a unified view of working, learning, and innovation. *Organization Science 2*(1): 40–57

Byrne-Jiménez, M., & Orr, M. T. (2004, April). *The nature of learning in principal collaborative inquiry: Implications for professional development.* Presentation at the Annual American Educational Research Association Conference.

Clandinin, D. J., & Connelly, F. M. (1995). *Teacher professional knowledge landscapes.* New York: Teachers College Press.

Clandinin, D. J., & Connelly, F. M. (2000). *Narrative inquiry: Experience and story in qualitative research.* San Francisco: Jossey-Bass.

Cooperrider, D., & Whitney, D. (2005). *Appreciative inquiry: A positive revolution in change.* San Francisco: Berrett-Koehler.

Craciun, K., & Snow-Renner, R. (2002). *No Child Left Behind Policy Brief: Low-performing schools.* Denver, CO: Education Commission of the States.

Crosby, E. A. (1999). Urban schools force to fail. *Phi Delta Kappan, 81*(4), 298–303.

Daresh, J., & Playko, M. (1992). *The professional development of school administrators.* Boston: Allyn & Bacon.

Darling-Hammond, L. (1997). What matters most: 21st-century teaching. *Education Digest, 63*(3).

DuFour, R., & Eaker, R. (1998). *Professional learning communities at work: Best practices for enhancing student achievement.* Bloomington, IN: Solution Tree.

Fiore, T. A., & Curtin, T. R. (1997, April). Public and private school principals in the United States: A Statistical profile, 1987–88 to 1993–94. Washington, DC: NCES.

Fullan, M. (1991). *The new meaning of educational change.* New York: Teachers College Press.

Garet, M. S., Porter, A. C., Desimone, L., Birman, B. F., & Yoon, K. S. (2001). What makes professional development effective? Results from a national sample of teachers. *American Educational Research Journal, 38*(4), 915–945.

Grace, A. (1996). Taking a critical pose: Andragogy—missing links, missing values. *International Journal of Lifelong Education, 15*(5), 382–392.

Greenwood, D. J., & Levin, M. (1998). *Introduction to action research.* Thousand Oaks, CA: Sage.

Hall, G. E., & Hord, S. M. (2001). *Implementing change: Patterns, principles, and potholes.* Boston: Allyn and Bacon.

Hallinger, P., & Wimpelberg, R. (1992). New settings and changing norms for principal development. *The Urban Review, 24*(1), 1–21.

Hart, A. W. (1993). *Principal succession: Establishing leadership in schools.* Albany, NY: State University of New York Press.

Heifetz, R., & Linsky, M. (2001). *Leadership on the line: Staying alive through the dangers of leading.* Cambridge, MA: Harvard Business School Press.

Heron, J. (1971). *Experience and method: an inquiry into the concept of experiential research.* Guilford, England: Human Potential Research Project, University of Surrey.

Heron, J. (1981). Philosophical Basis for a New Paradigm. In P. Reason & J. Rowan (Eds.), *Human inquiry: A source book of new paradigm research* (pp. 19–36). Chichester, UK: John Wiley & Sons.

Heron, J. (1996). *Co-operative inquiry: Research into the human condition.* London: Sage.

Heron, J., & Reason, P. (2001). Practice of co-operative inquiry: Research "with" rather than "on" people. In P. Reason & H. Bradbury (Eds.), *Handbook of action research: Participative inquiry and practice* (pp. 179–188). London: Sage.

Hugo, J. M. (2002). Learning community history. *New Directions for Adult Learning, 95,* 5–25.

Institute for Educational Leadership. (2000). *Leadership for student learning: Principal leadership.* Washington, DC: IEL Report.

Knowles, M. S. (1962). *The adult education movement in the United States.* New York: Holt, Rinehart, & Winston.

Knowles, M. S. (1978). Gearing up for the eighties. *Training and Development Journal, 32*(7), 12–14.

Krueger, R. A. (1994). *Focus groups.* Thousand Oaks, CA: Sage.

Lave, J., & Wenger, E. (1991). *Situated learning: Legitimate peripheral participation.* Cambridge: Cambridge University Press.

Learning First Alliance. (2003, March). *Beyond islands of excellence: What districts can do to improve instruction and achievement in all schools—A leadership brief.* Retrieved May 9, 2006, from www.learningfirst.org.

Leithwood, K., & Jantzi, D. (1999). The relative effects of principal and teacher sources of leadership on student engagement with school. *Educational Administration Quarterly, 35,* 679–706.

Leithwood, K., & Riehl, C (2003, August). *What we know about successful school leadership.* Retrieved October 2, 2006, from http://www.cepa.gse.rutgers.edu/ whatweknow.pdf#search=%22leithwood%20riehl%22.

Leithwood, K., & Steinbach, R. (1995). *Expert problem solving.* Albany, NY: SUNY Press.

Lieberman, A., & Grolnick, M. (1997). Networks, reform, and the professional development of teachers. In A. Hargreaves (Ed.), *Rethinking educational change with heart and mind* (pp. 192–215). Alexandria, VA: Association for Supervision and Curriculum Development.

Marsick, V. (2002). *Action learning conversation.* Partners for Learning and Leadership. www.partnersforlearning.com.

McCauley, C. D., Moxley, R. S., & Van Velsor, E. (1998). *Handbook of leadership development* (pp. 1–25). San Francisco: Jossey-Bass.

McDonald, J. P., Mohr, N., Dichter, A., & McDonald, E. C. (2003). *The power of protocols.* New York: Teachers College Press.

Merriam, S. (2001). Andragogy and self-directed learning: Pillars of adult learning theory. *The New Update on Adult Learning Theory, 89,* 3–13.

Mezirow, J. (1991). *Transformative dimensions of adult learning.* San Francisco: Jossey-Bass.

Mezirow, J. (2000). Learning to think like an adult. In J. Mezirow & Associates (Eds.), *Learning as transformation: Critical perspectives on a theory in progress.* San Francisco, CA: Jossey-Bass.

Miles, M. B., & Huberman, M. A. (1994). *Qualitative analysis: An expanded sourcebook* (2nd ed.). Thousand Oaks, CA: Sage.

National Center for Educational Statistics (NCES). (2001). *School and staffing survey, 1999–2000.* Washington, DC: Author.

Neufeld, B. (1997). Responding to the expressed needs of urban middle school principals. *Urban Education, 31*(5), 490–510.

Orr, M. T., Byrne-Jiménez, M., McFarlane, P., & Brown, B. (2005). Leading out from low-performing: Learning to and transforming through the urban principalship. *Leadership and Policy in Schools, 4,* 23–54.

Osterman, K., & Sullivan, S. (1996, November). New principals in an urban bureaucracy: A sense of efficacy. *Journal of School Leadership, 6,* 661–690.

Osterman, K. F., & Kottkamp, R. B. (2004). *Reflective practice for educators.* Thousand Oaks, CA: Corwin Press.

Parkay, F. W., Currie, G. D., & Rhodes, J. W. (1992). Professional socialization: A longitudinal study of first-time high school principals. *Educational Administration Quarterly, 28*(1), 43–75.

Peterson, K. (2001). *The professional development of principals: Innovations and opportunities.* Paper Commissioned for the First Meeting of the National Council for the Advancement of Educational Leadership Preparation.

Portin, B. (2000). The changing urban principalship. *Education and Urban Society, 32*(4), 492–505.

Price, J. (1999). *Crisis in leadership: Finding and keeping educational leaders for New York City's Public Schools.* New York: New Visions for Public Schools.

Reason, P. (Ed.). (1988). *Human inquiry in action*. London: Sage.

Reason, P. (Ed.). (1994). *Participation in human inquiry*. London: Sage.

Sagor, R. (1992). *How to conduct collaborative action research*. Alexandria, VA: Association for Supervision and Curriculum Development.

Schön, D. (1987). *The reflective practitioner*. New York: Basic Books.

Shen, J., Rodriguez-Campos, L., & Rincones-Gomez, R. (2000). Characteristics of urban principalship: A national trend study. *Education and Urban Society, 32*(4), 481–491.

Strauss, A., & Corbin, J. (1990). *Basics of qualitative research*. London: Sage.

Walker, E., Mitchel, C., & Turner, W. (1999). *Professional development and urban leadership: A study of urban administrators' perceptions of what matters most in their professional development*. Paper presented at the annual meeting of the American Educational Research Association, Montreal, Canada.

Waters, J., Marzano, R., & McNulty, B. (2003). *Balanced leadership: What 30 years of research tells us about the effect of leadership on student achievement*. Aurora, CO: Mid-continent Research for Education and Learning.

Wenger, E. (1998). *Communities of practice: Learning, meaning and identity*. Cambridge, England: Cambridge University Press.

Wheatley, M. (2000). Goodbye, command and control. In *The Jossey-Bass reader on education leadership* (pp. 339–347). San Francisco: Jossey-Bass.

Yin, R. K. (2002). *Case study research: Design and methods* (3rd ed.). Thousand Oaks, CA: Sage.

Index

Note: CI refers to collaborative inquiry.

About the Authors

Mónica Byrne-Jiménez, EdD, is a faculty member of the Department of Foundations, Leadership and Policy Studies, in the School of Education and Allied Human Services at Hofstra University. Her interests are in leadership development among principals and early career superintendents, professional development as a vehicle for school improvement, and the role of facilitators in fostering adult learning. Her work has been published in the *Leadership and Policy in Schools* journal and other online sources.

Margaret Terry Orr, PhD, is on the faculty of Bank Street College, where she directs the Future School Leaders Academy, a university–district partnership program with 17 suburban school districts, and is co-founder of a New York City–focused school improvement initiative. Her primary work is in strengthening formal leadership preparation programs through evaluation, research, and demonstration initiatives, and in principal and superintendent leadership development. Her research has been published in the *Educational Administration Quarterly, Phi Delta Kappan, Teachers College Record, Leadership and Policy in Schools, Education and Urban Society*, and other research journals and books.